GOD'S PROPHETIC TIMELINE

Messiah's Final Warning

CHADWICK HARVEY

GOD'S PROPHETIC
TIMELINE

Copyright © 2016 by Chadwick Harvey

World Ahead Press is a division of WND Books. The views and opinions expressed in this book are those of the author and do not necessarily reflect the official policy or position or WND Books.

Paperback ISBN: 978-1-944212-44-5
eBook ISBN: 978-1-944212-45-2

Printed in the United States of America
16 17 18 19 20 21 LSI 9 8 7 6 5 4 3 2 1

DEDICATED TO

All of the faithful and watchful saints who will understand the time of the Lord's visitation. Keep fighting the good fight of the faith, taking hold of eternal life. May God bless and protect all of you.

CONTENTS

ACKNOWLEDGMENTS

First and foremost, all glory, honor, and credit goes to God Almighty, Jesus the Messiah, and the Holy Spirit (Holy Trinity), from whom all blessings come, according to His will. Without His everlasting love, mercy, grace, forgiveness, inspiration, and guidance, this book would have never been written. I love Him with all of my heart, soul, mind, and strength, forever and ever. His Kingdom come, His will be done. Amen.

I would like to give a special thanks to my family, whose love, support, and prayers have encouraged me to write this book. God has blessed me with a phenomenal family, and I thank Him for each of you.

Last, I would like to thank my friends and the Faithful Performance Community for your support, inspiration, and feedback. May God bless all of you!

INTRODUCTION

ARE WE THE TERMINAL GENERATION?

The most imperative and profound question of today is, "Are we the generation to witness the Second Coming of Jesus the Messiah?" When God became flesh and fulfilled His divine appointments at His First Coming, He blessed mankind with His salvation, Jesus! Since that prophetic moment in history, every generation has believed that it would witness Messiah's Second Coming. Throughout the centuries, Bible scholars and prophecy teachers have examined the Holy Scriptures in search for the revelations concerning the time when the terminal generation would live to see Messiah's return to Earth. Today, our generation is not any different, because some Bible scholars and prophecy teachers believe that we are living at the end of the age, which will conclude with Jesus' glorious appearing (Matt. 24).

Are the "beginning of sorrows" occurring today in our generation as Messiah prophesied in Matthew 24? As believers, when we take a sober look around the globe, needless to say, we can see the prophetic puzzle coming together year after year and moment by moment. If we pay close attention to the end of the age teachings of Messiah and the Biblical prophets, we can feel the intensity of those warnings occurring with more and more velocity than ever before in history.

Even nonbelievers and secularists are declaring that there is a massive change that is about to occur on the Earth, whether it is global warming, climate change, or the latest "worldly proclaimed catastrophe." Additionally, the mainstream media and Hollywood have "tuned our ears" to apocalyptic terms and movies such as, *Armageddon, World War III, Global Economic Meltdown, Apocalypse, Post World, Social Collapse,* and *The End Times.* Both groups have also routinely mocked the Word of God (2 Thess. 2) by foolishly not understanding God's holy scriptures.

Furthermore, the apostle Paul tells us that God's creation groans and labors as it eagerly waits for its deliverance, in hope of its release from the bondage of corruption into the glorious liberty of its beginning state (Rom. 8:18–25).

Without question, we are living at a unique moment in time where believers and nonbelievers alike can agree on one thing; our generation is living in the most exciting juncture in the history of the world! With that being said, there is an overwhelming majority of believers who do not understand God's prophetic timeline, or the kingdoms and events that have occurred, are occurring, and will occur in the future. Unfortunately, as a whole, there is not an urgent calling and revival towards one goal: proclaiming God's prophetic timeline for Messiah's Second Coming!

In the Holy Bible, Messiah and the prophets warned mankind about the specific signs, kingdoms, and events that would precisely occur in the generation of His Second Coming, which is also known as the great and awesome day of the Lord (Joel 2:32). As believers, we have been blessed with the Word of God to explore and discover the wisdom, knowledge, and understanding of God's prophetic timeline. Make no mistake, Messiah Himself commanded us to watch (Mark 13:35–36), so that we will be called wise and faithful servants (Matt. 25). As faithful servants, we are called to be the light of the world, the salt of the earth (Matt. 5), and to fulfill the Great Commission (Matthew 28:19–20). As followers of Messiah, it is our duty to share God's prophetic timeline of Messiah's Second Coming with all of mankind, and at the same time warn of His future judgment on the Earth, as well (Rev. 6–19).

So, let us ask ourselves these imperative and profound questions; "Are we the terminal generation that was prophesied thousands of years ago to witness Messiah's Second Coming? Are there prophecies in the Holy Bible that explains God's prophetic timeline and the kingdoms and events that will lead up to His glorious appearing? Are we living at the end of the age before Messiah's Second Coming and millennial reign on Earth?"

In God's prophetic timeline, we will discover the answers to these important questions by exploring the Biblical prophecies written as far back as four thousand years ago, which will navigate us in our understanding of the current kingdom that our generation is living in today! God's prophets will also declare what kingdoms and events that will occur in the future, as we journey towards our final destination. In this book, we will also reveal the region of the ten kings of the Antichrist's kingdom, and we will discover what country is called "Mystery Babylon."

From that point, our journey will continue with Messiah's Second Coming, His millennial reign, and the New Jerusalem, and it will conclude with Messiah's final warning. When we reach our final destination, we will have a definitive confirmation of God's prophetic timeline and the Second Coming events of the King of Kings and Lord of Lords, Jesus the Messiah!

Before we begin this prophetic journey, it is important to realize why Biblical prophecy is so crucial for us to understand. The apostle John, author of the book of Revelation, declares, "for the testimony of Jesus is the spirit of prophecy" (Rev. 19:10). Certainly, this tells us that the testimony of Messiah to mankind should definitely include the prophecies He fulfilled at His First Coming, and also the prophecies that He will fulfill at His Second Coming and millennial reign. Clearly, the Almighty wants us to understand what prophecies Messiah has and will fulfill, so that we will have great wisdom and knowledge concerning His Second Coming and millennial reign. Now, without further delay, let us begin our journey on God's prophetic timeline!

CHAPTER 1

THE TERMINAL GENERATION

There are two nonnegotiable prophecies that had to be fulfilled before Messiah's Second Coming; Israel had to become a nation again, and the children of Israel had to recapture Jerusalem as their capital. The fulfillment of these two prophecies would escalate and intensify God's prophetic timeline unto the Day of the Lord, Messiah's Second Coming. The prophet Isaiah gives us great insight concerning both prophecies, as we will discover throughout this chapter.

1948 PROPHECY

Isaiah 66:8, "Who has heard such a thing? Who has seen such things? Shall the earth be made to give birth in one day? Or shall a nation be born at once?"

After approximately 1,900 years from the destruction of Jerusalem in AD 70, the nation of Israel was "born again" in 1948, fulfilling Isaiah's prophecy. How did this prophetic event occur?

On November 5, 1914, during World War I, the British Empire declared war on the Ottoman Empire (Muslim) who controlled Jerusalem and occupied the Promised Land (Israel). On November 2, 1917, the United Kingdom's Foreign Secretary Arthur James Balfour sent a letter to Walter Rothschild, who was one of the leaders of the British Jewish community. Rothschild submitted the declaration to the Zionist Federation of Great Britain and Ireland. This declaration letter became known as the Balfour Declaration. In 1917, which was a jubilee year (Leviticus 25), the Balfour Declaration became the first official step in fulfilling the 1948 prophecy. In the letter below, we can see the declaration of the British Empire's efforts to restore the children of Israel to the Promised Land.

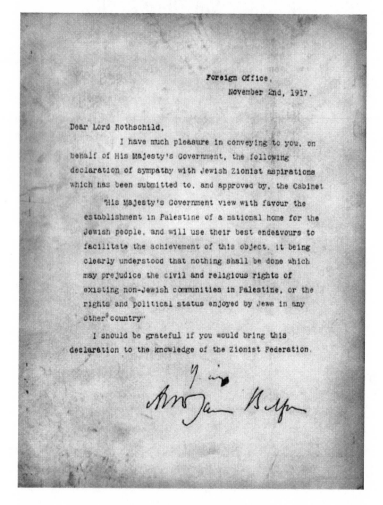

Balfour Declaration-Public Record

In 1917, at the pinnacle of World War I, General Allenby of the British Empire captured a region of the Promised Land from the Ottoman Empire, ending four hundred years of Muslim control. As the war ended and the Ottoman Empire declined in power, the League of Nations divided the Promised Land between Israel and the Arabs. However, once the declaration was executed, the children of Israel were allocated approximately twenty percent of the land promised to them by God in the Abrahamic Covenant (Gen. 15), *excluding* Jerusalem. The remainder of the Promised Land was given to the Arabs. Please note, although the children of Israel will not inherit all of the Promised Land from God until Messiah returns for His Second Coming and millennial reign, twenty percent was a very small portion compared to what the Arabs received (eighty percent). Nevertheless, the 1917 Balfour Declaration was the first official step for the children of Israel to regain control of the Promised Land in 1948.

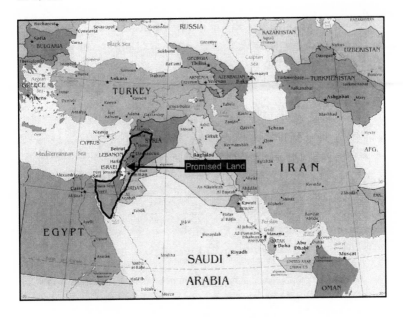

Promised Land-Free map from biblesnet.com

On May 14, 1948, Israel became a nation again and fulfilled Isaiah's prophecy! Biblical prophecies have been fulfilled throughout history; however, this was the most important prophecy since Messiah fulfilled the prophecies of His First Coming events. This is absolutely incredible, because Israel is the only nation to have accomplished such a calling and mission. Only by God Almighty's right hand and divine intervention did His heritage, His land, Israel, fulfill Isaiah's prophetic words. America, Britain, and the United Nations can take credit for acting on Israel's behalf, but it was God Almighty's influence among men that enabled Israel to become a nation again (Dan. 2:20–21). The 1948 Prophecy is the foundation of all of the other end of the age prophecies, as it is the key that opens the door for the prophecies to be fulfilled. As we continue, Isaiah also gives us great insight of the next prophetic event on God's prophetic timeline, the 1967 prophecy.

> Isaiah 66:8–9, "For as soon as Zion (Jerusalem) was in labor, she gave birth to her children. Shall I bring to the time of birth, and not cause delivery?" says the Lord. Shall I who cause delivery shut up the womb?" says your God."

1967 PROPHECY

After the prophetic fulfillment of Israel becoming a nation again in 1948, the next major event to be fulfilled on God's prophetic timeline was Israel's recapturing and controlling of the holy city of Jerusalem. As we discussed, the children of Israel did not receive the rights from the League of Nations to control Jerusalem when it became a nation again in 1948. So, they would have to conquer the holy city in order to fulfill Isaiah's prophecy.

> Matthew 23:39, "For I say to you, you shall see Me no more (Second Coming) till you say, 'Blessed is He who comes in the name of the Lord."

Messiah also prophesied that the children of Israel would rule over Jerusalem before His Second Coming. He confirms that the children of Israel will be in Jerusalem by stating that they would not see Him again until they proclaimed the famous words, "Blessed is He who comes in the name of the Lord," in Jerusalem. Messiah declared this prophecy as He was standing on the Mount of Olives (Jerusalem), which is the exact location where He will place His feet at His Second Coming (Zech. 14:3–4). Now, let us explore the book of Psalms to confirm the great significance of the 1967 prophecy.

Psalm 102:16,18, "For the Lord shall build up Zion; He shall appear in His glory. This is written for the generation to come."

This prophecy declares that once the Lord builds up Zion (Jerusalem), He will appear in His glory. For approximately nineteen hundred years (AD 70–1966), the children of Israel (Jews) did not control the holy city, therefore the Lord did not "build up Zion." However, in June of 1967, during the Six-Day War, the children of Israel recaptured Zion. And since that time, the Lord has built up Jerusalem in all aspects of the world (Hebrew language, science, natural resources, military, medicine (cures for diseases), settlements, desert blossoming like a rose, et cetera).

The prophecy continues to proclaim, "this is written for the generation to come." The Hebrew word for "generation to come" is *acharon* (*Strong's* #314), which means *terminal or last*. To paraphrase Psalm 102:16, 18, "When the Lord builds up Zion (Jerusalem), He shall appear in His glory. This is written for the terminal or last generation." In other words, the prophecy is declaring that once the Lord builds up Jerusalem (Zion), He will appear at His Second Coming!

HOW WAS THE 1967 PROPHECY FULFILLED?

Fifty years after the 1917 Balfour Declaration, in the jubilee year of 1967, Israeli soldiers entered the Lion's gate (Eastern gate) and recaptured Jerusalem as their capital for the first time in approximately 1,900 years! Israel defeated five countries in order to win the Six-Day War; Egypt, Jordan, Syria, Iraq, and Lebanon. These five countries had the additional support of Algeria, Saudi Arabia, Libya, Kuwait, Pakistan, Morocco, Sudan, Tunisia, and the PLO. Nineteen short years after becoming a nation again, Israel conquered Jerusalem in the Six-Day War and rested on the Sabbath, fulfilling this prophecy on God's prophetic timeline. Only by God Almighty's divine intervention and sovereign righteousness can a nation, who only had nineteen years to establish itself and train its own military, defeat all five of those countries. Hallelujah!

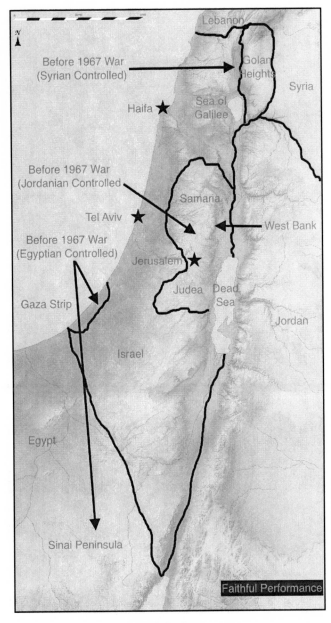

Pre 1967 Borders

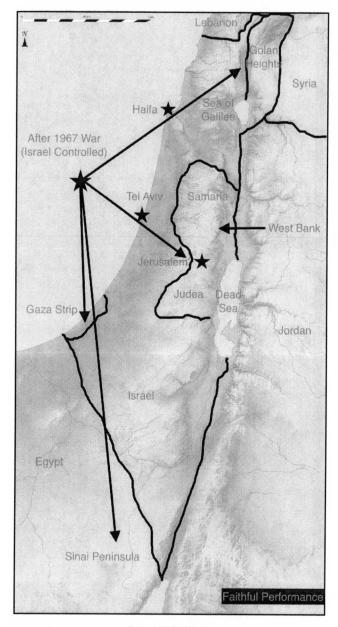

Post 1967 Borders

The fulfillment of the 1948 and 1967 prophecies occurred through God Almighty's intervention on His prophetic timeline in order for His superior plan to be fulfilled. Neither human hands nor armies of mortal men could have accomplished these two events without His divine intercession. These two prophecies had to be fulfilled before all of the other end of the age prophecies could be fulfilled. However, the lingering question remains, "What is a generation?"

At Messiah's First Coming, as He journeyed to the Mount of Olives to prophesy about the warning signs of the end of the age (Olivet Discourse), He proclaimed the following:

> Matthew 23:36–38, "*Assuredly, I say to you, all these things will come upon this generation.* "O Jerusalem, Jerusalem, the one who kills the prophets and stones those who are sent to her! How often I wanted to gather your children together, as a hen gathers her chicks under her wings, but you were not willing! See! *Your house is left to you desolate.*"

> Matthew 24:1–2, "Then Jesus went out and departed from the temple, and His disciples came up to show Him the buildings of the temple. *And Jesus said to them, "Do you not see all these things? Assuredly, I say to you, not one stone shall be left here upon another, that shall not be thrown down.*"

In Matthew 23, Messiah scolded the religious leaders as hypocrites for their blasphemous, murderous ways toward the prophets, and also for not understanding the "time of their visitation" (Luke 19:41–44). He also gives us wisdom and knowledge of the approximate length of a generation. Messiah prophesied that Jerusalem would be left desolate, as one stone would not be left on top of another or not thrown down. He was prophesying about the Roman destruction and exile that was fulfilled in AD 70.

WHAT CAN WE MAKE OF THIS PROPHECY?

Messiah was crucified and resurrected in approximately AD 30–33, so His prophecy of the Roman destruction and exile was fulfilled approximately forty years later. This confirms that when the Holy Bible declares "this generation," it refers to the generation who the prophecy is given for, and in that case, was the generation of AD 30–33, but in the 1967 prophecy (Psalm 102:16, 18), it refers to the 1967 generation. Moses also tells us the approximate length of a generation, as well.

Psalm 90:10, "The days of our lives are seventy years; And if by reason of strength they are eighty years."

These two examples give us great insight as to how God defines a generation, as an entire generation, not an individual, will not exceed eighty years, according to the Scriptures.

CONCLUSION

Please note, I am not prophesying or setting dates in any way. However, it is imperative for us to understand where our generation is on God's prophetic timeline, so that we can proclaim the good news!

Once Israel became a nation again in 1948, and when the children of Israel recaptured Jerusalem as their capital in 1967, God's prophetic timeline for the end of the age prophecies began to be fulfilled before His Second Coming events. Furthermore, in Isaiah 66, after Isaiah prophesied about Israel becoming a nation again (1948) and the children of Israel recapturing Jerusalem (1967), he concludes his prophecy by declaring the Second Coming of Messiah, the millennial reign, and the New Jerusalem in sequential order! Is this a coincidence or was Isaiah giving us wisdom and knowledge of God's prophetic timeline?

Isaiah 66:14–16, "*When you see this,* your heart shall rejoice, and your bones shall flourish like grass; the hand of the Lord shall be known to His servants, and His indignation to His enemies. *For behold, the Lord will come with fire and with His chariots, like a whirlwind, to render His anger with fury, and His rebuke with flames of fire. For by fire and by His sword the Lord will judge all flesh; and the slain of the Lord shall be many.*"

CHAPTER 2

THE VISION OF A RAM AND A GOAT

The book of Daniel is one of the most prophetic and symbolic books in the Holy Bible. It gives us great wisdom, knowledge, and understanding of God's prophetic timeline and how the kingdoms and events will unfold at the end of the age. Throughout his incredible book, Daniel prophesies about the major kingdoms that will reign on the Earth before Messiah's Second Coming by using symbolism of metal components and animals. Once we understand the symbolism of the kingdoms, along with their historical context, we will gain great insight about who they are, when they will rise to power, and what kingdom our generation is living in today on God's prophetic timeline. In the next several chapters, we will explore and discover these amazing prophecies of Daniel as we continue our journey on God's prophetic timeline. Now, let us begin with the vision of Daniel 8.

Daniel 8:1–4, "In the third year of the reign of King Belshazzar a vision appeared to me—to me, Daniel—after the one that appeared to me the first time. I saw in the vision, and it so happened while I was looking, that I was in Shushan, the citadel, which is in the province of Elam; and I saw in the vision that I was by the River Ulai. Then I lifted my eyes and saw, and there, standing beside the river, was a ram which had two horns, and the two horns were high; but one was higher than the other, and the higher one came up last. I saw the ram pushing westward, northward, and southward, so that no animal could withstand him; nor was there any that could deliver from his hand, but he did according to his will and became great."

In the latter years of the ancient Babylonian Empire, under Belshazzar's reign (550–539 BC), Daniel received a vision from the Lord. Daniel's vision begins in Elam, which is modern-day Iran (Persia), where he saw a ram with two horns, with one horn higher than the other. Most Bible scholars and prophecy teachers agree that the ram symbolizes the ancient Medo-Persian Empire (Kurds-Iran). The higher horn represents Persia (Iran), because it was the dominant power between the two. Daniel proclaims that the ram (Persia) conquered westward, northward, and southward, and became a great and dominant power. Just as Daniel prophesied, history will prove that the Medo-Persian Empire conquered a large area of the ancient world.

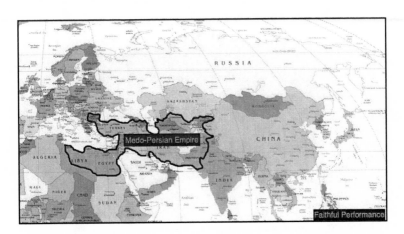

Medo-Persian Empire

Daniel 8:5–7, "And as I was considering, suddenly a male goat came from the west, across the surface of the whole earth, without touching the ground; and the goat had a notable horn between his eyes. Then he came to the ram that had two horns, which I had seen standing beside the river, and ran at him with furious power. And I saw him confronting the ram; he was moved with rage against him, attacked the ram, and broke his two horns. There was no power in the ram to withstand him, but he cast him down to the ground and trampled him; and there was no one that could deliver the ram from his hand."

As Daniel was considering the dominance of the two-horned ram (Medo-Persia), he saw a male goat coming from the west with a notable horn between his eyes. Daniel explains that the male goat raged against the ram, breaking his two horns and destroying him. Most Bible scholars and prophecy teachers conclude that the male goat symbolizes the Grecian Empire, with its leader, Alexander the Great, representing the "notable horn." History will also prove that the goat, the Grecian Empire, conquered and destroyed the ram with two horns, the Medo-Persian Empire.

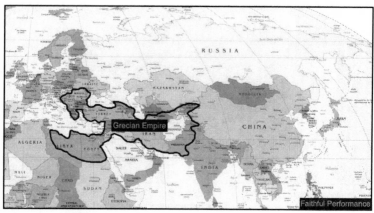

Grecian Empire

26

As Daniel finished speaking about the destruction of the ram (Medo-Persia) by the goat (Greece), he gives us additional details about the Grecian Empire.

Daniel 8:8–12, "Therefore the male goat grew very great; but when he became strong, the large horn was broken, and in place of it four notable ones came up toward the four winds of heaven. And out of one of them came a little horn which grew exceedingly great toward the south, toward the east, and toward the Glorious Land. And it grew up to the host of heaven; and it cast down some of the host and some of the stars to the ground, and trampled them. He even exalted himself as high as the Prince of the host; and by him the daily sacrifices were taken away, and the place of His sanctuary was cast down. Because of transgression, an army was given over to the horn to oppose the daily sacrifices; and he cast truth down to the ground. He did all this and prospered."

Daniel explains that after the male goat (Grecian Empire) became great, his large horn broke, which refers to the end of his reign. Once the large horn broke (died), the Grecian Empire would divide into four regions (four horns). Most Bible scholars and prophecy teachers agree that the "four horns" which came up after the large horn broke are four of the regions that the Grecian Empire divided into after Alexander died; Seleucus-North, Ptolemy-South, Cassander-West, Lysimachus-East.

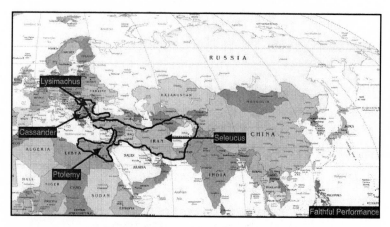

Four Divisions of the Grecian Empire

Daniel continues to describe a "little horn" that came out of the four horns (regions) of the Grecian Empire that "grew exceedingly great toward the south and toward the east, including the Promised Land." He is prophesying of the future Antichrist (Satan incarnate), because the horn "grew up to the host of heaven and cast down some of the host and some of the stars from heaven, exalting himself as high as the Prince of Host." Daniel also declares that the little horn (Antichrist) will end the daily sacrifices at that time. Isaiah and John confirm Daniel's prophecies of the Antichrist, because they give the same description and actions of the son of perdition as found in Daniel 8.

> Isaiah 14:14, "I will ascend above the heights of the clouds, I will be like the Most High."

> Revelation 12:4, "His tail drew a third of the stars of heaven and threw them to the earth."

> Daniel 9:27, "But in the middle of the week he shall bring an end to sacrifice and offering."

At first glance, Daniel 8 seems as if it has been fulfilled by the ancient Medo-Persian and Grecian Empires, except for the little horn (Antichrist) and his kingdom. However, is Daniel 8 an end of the age prophecy? Could the events of this chapter have been a prophetic foreshadow of what is to come in the future?

> Daniel 8:15–19, "Then it happened, when I, Daniel, had seen the vision and was seeking the meaning, that suddenly there stood before me one having the appearance of a man. And I heard a man's voice between the banks of the Ulai, who called, and said, "Gabriel, make this man understand the vision." So he came near where I stood, and when he came I was afraid and fell on my face; but he said to me, *"Understand, son of man, that the vision refers to the time of the end."* Now, as he was speaking with me, I was in a deep sleep with my face to the ground; but he touched me, and stood me upright. And he said, *"Look, I am making known to you what shall happen in the latter time of the indignation; for at the appointed time the end shall be."*

As Daniel pondered the meaning of the vision, God's angel Gabriel was commanded to make Daniel understand this prophecy. Gabriel told Daniel *three times* that Daniel 8 is a vision for the end of the age!

1. "Understand, son of man, that the vision refers to the time of the end."
2. "Look, I am making known to you what shall happen in the latter time of the indignation."
3. "For at the appointed time the end shall be."

Gabriel emphatically tells Daniel three times that Daniel 8 is an end of the age prophecy. We have to understand that the time of the end is truly "the time of the end." The ancient Medo-Persian and

Grecian Empires ruled approximately 2,500 years ago, so obviously it was not the time of the end. It is very important to understand this next fact. Often times, God inspired the prophets to prophesy through current events and events shortly thereafter, to give us prophetic foreshadows in order for us to understand what events will occur in the future. As the famous saying goes, history repeats itself, and so does the Holy Bible.

> Ecclesiastes 1:9, "That which has been is what will be, that which is done is what will be done, *and there is nothing new under the sun.*"

> Isaiah 46:9–10, "Remember the former things of old, for I am God, and there is no other; I am God, and there is none like Me, *declaring the end from the beginning, and from ancient times things that are not yet done.*"

Although Daniel 8 parallels world history, Gabriel definitely proclaims that the vision is for the end of the age. As we continue exploring the interpretation of Daniel 8, Gabriel confirms who the two kingdoms are that will rise to power at the end of the age, and he also gives us further confirmation that this prophecy will occur at the time of the end.

> Daniel 8:20–26, "The ram which you saw, having the two horns, they are the kings of Media and Persia. And the male goat is the kingdom of Greece. The large horn that is between its eyes is the first king. As for the broken horn and the four that stood up in its place, four kingdoms shall arise out of that nation, but not with its power. "And in the latter time of their kingdom, when the transgressors have reached their fullness, a king shall arise, having fierce features, who understands sinister schemes. His power shall be mighty, but not by his own power; He shall destroy fearfully, and shall

prosper and thrive; He shall destroy the mighty, and also the holy people. "Through his cunning he shall cause deceit to prosper under his rule; And he shall exalt himself in his heart. He shall destroy many in their prosperity. He shall even rise against the Prince of princes; But he shall be broken without human means. "And the vision of the evenings and mornings which was told is true; Therefore, seal up the vision, for it refers to many days in the future."

At the end of the interpretation of Daniel 8, Gabriel tells Daniel to "seal up this vision, for it refers to many days in the future," which is another confirmation that Daniel 8 is an end of the age prophecy. Gabriel confirms that the ram is the Medo-Persian Empire (Iran), and the goat is the Grecian Empire (Turkey). He prophesies that once the large horn (first king) fulfills God's prophetic timeline, he will die (broken horn), and the Grecian Empire (Turkey) will be divided into four regions. Once this comes to pass at the end of the age (latter time), the Antichrist (little horn) will rise from the Grecian Empire and wage war against the holy people and the Prince of princes, Messiah. The descriptions that Gabriel uses about "the king" clearly points to the Antichrist (Satan incarnate):

- Fierce features and sinister schemes (Dan. 11:34)
- Power shall be mighty, but not by his own power (2 Thess. 2:9)
- He shall prosper and destroy the mighty and holy people (Dan. 7:25, 11:39)
- He will be cunning (Gen. 3:1)
- He shall exalt himself in his heart (Isa. 14:12–15, Ezek. 28:2,17)
- He shall rise against the Prince of princes (Messiah) (Dan. 7:25, 11:36)

In Daniel 8, it is very clear that Gabriel gave Daniel and future generations (you and me), wisdom, knowledge, and understanding of the prophetic foreshadows of the ancient Medo-Persian and Grecian Empires. If Daniel 8 is a vision of the end of the age, then we can conclude that the Medo-Persian (Iran) and Grecian Empires (Turkey) will rise to power after the 1948 and 1967 prophecies, and then the Antichrist (little horn) will rise from one of the four regions of the ancient Grecian Empire (Daniel 8:9). Out of the four regions of the Grecian Empire, from which region will the Antichrist arise?

> Daniel 8:8–9, "Therefore the male goat grew very great; but when he became strong, the large horn was broken, and in place of it four notable ones came up toward the four winds of heaven. And out of one of them came a little horn which grew exceedingly great toward the south, toward the east, and toward the Glorious Land."

As we discovered, at the end of the age, the Grecian Empire will be divided into four regions. Daniel prophesies that a little horn (Antichrist) will rise from one of the regions, and he will "grow great toward the south, the east, and towards the Glorious Land" (Israel). If the little horn (Antichrist) grows "toward the south," he must be coming from the north. This tells us that the Antichrist will rise from the northern region of the Grecian Empire, which is the Seleucid division. In Daniel 11, he also calls the Antichrist the "King of the North" (Dan. 11:40), which also confirms this region, as well. Please note, geographically, Turkey (Grecian Empire) is directly north of Israel, the Glorious Land.

Grecian Empire

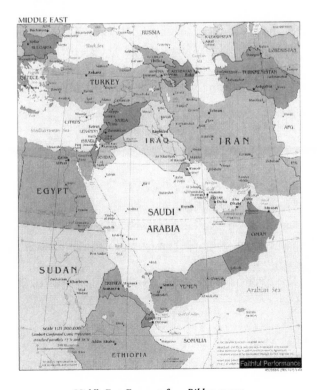

Middle East-Free map from Biblesnet.com

Additionally, Messiah also confirms that the Antichrist will rise from the Seleucid division.

Revelation 2:12–13, "These things says He who has the sharp two- edged sword: *"I know your works, and where you dwell, where Satan's throne is.* And you hold fast to My name, and did not deny My faith even in the days in which Antipas was My faithful martyr, who was killed among you, *where Satan dwells."*

In this Scripture, Messiah is speaking to the church at Pergamum, which was located in the ancient Seleucid division of modern day Turkey. It is important to recognize that Messiah prophesies where Satan's throne is located, so we must note that He is saying *"is located,"* not "was located," so this is where Satan *"dwells,"* not "dwelled." Of course Satan "runs to and fro" all over the earth (See Job 1:7; John 12:31; John 14:30), but Messiah clearly tells us that Satan's (Antichrist) throne is located in the Seleucid region of Turkey.

CONCLUSION

The Order of Events in Daniel 8:

1. Medo-Persian Empire (Iran)
2. Grecian Empire (Turkey)
3. Large horn (leader) dies (large horn broken)
4. The Grecian Empire (Turkey) is divided into four divisions
5. The Little horn (Antichrist) rises out of the Seleucid division

CHAPTER 3

THE VISION OF THE FOUR BEASTS

D aniel 7, the vision of the four beasts, is also a revelation that Daniel received from the Lord in the latter years of the ancient Babylonian Empire under Belshazzar's reign (550–539 BC). This prophecy proclaims the four major kingdoms (beasts) that will rule on the earth before Messiah's Second Coming and millennial reign. Please note, just as Daniel 8 uses animals as symbolism for the kingdoms, so does Daniel 7.

Is Daniel 7 an end of the age prophecy? Do Daniel chapters 7 and 8 prophesy about three of the same kingdoms that will rise at the end of the age? Before we discover the answers to these imperative questions, let us review the kingdoms in Daniel 8.

DANIEL 8

1. Medo-Persian Empire- (Ram)
2. Grecian Empire- (Goat)
3. Antichrist's kingdom

Daniel 7:2–6, "Daniel spoke, saying, "I saw in my vision by night, and behold, the four winds of heaven were stirring up the Great Sea. And four great beasts came up from the sea, each different from the other. *The first was like a lion*, and had eagle's wings. I watched till its wings were plucked off; and it was lifted up from the earth and made to stand on two feet like a man, and a man's heart was given to it. *"And suddenly another beast, a second, like a bear.* It was raised up on one side, and had three ribs in its mouth between its teeth. And they said thus to it: 'Arise, devour much flesh!' *"After this I looked, and there was another, like a leopard,* which had on its back four wings of a bird. *The beast also had four heads, and dominion was given to it."*

Daniel 7's vision gives us a prophetic picture of four kingdoms that will rule on the Earth. Most Bible scholars and prophecy teachers agree that the first three kingdoms in the vision are as follows; Babylonian Empire (lion), Medo-Persian Empire (bear), and the Grecian Empire (leopard). History will prove that these kingdoms ruled after one another in ancient times. Just as the four horns in Daniel 8 represent the four regions of the ancient Grecian Empire after Alexander the Great died (Seleucus-North, Ptolemy-South, Cassander-West, Lysimachus-East), the four heads of the leopard (Grecian Empire) represent the same four regions.

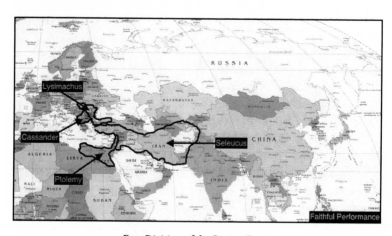

Four Divisions of the Grecian Empire

DANIEL 7'S BEASTS (KINGDOMS)

1. Lion - Babylonian Empire
2. Bear - Medo-Persian Empire
3. Leopard - Grecian Empire/ Four Regions of Grecian Empire
4. ?

Daniel 7:7–8, "After this I saw in the night visions, and behold, *a fourth beast, dreadful and terrible, exceedingly strong. It had huge iron teeth; it was devouring, breaking in pieces, and trampling the residue with its feet.* It was different from all the beasts that were before it, and it had ten horns. *I was considering the horns, and there was another horn, a little one, coming up among them*, before whom three of the first horns were plucked out by the roots. *And there, in this horn, were eyes like the eyes of a man, and a mouth speaking pompous words.*"

Daniel continues his prophecy by describing the fourth beast as dreadful and terrible, and exceedingly strong with iron teeth. He explains that the fourth beast is different from the first three beasts, and it had ten horns (We will discover the ten horns of the beast in a later chapter). Daniel also states that while he was considering the ten horns of the beast, a little horn came up from among the ten horns, having the eyes of a man, and he spoke blasphemous pompous words. Just as in Daniel 8, the little horn in Daniel 7 symbolizes the Antichrist, and he will rule over the ten kings (horns), as he "came up among them and plucked three of the kings (horns) out by the roots." In other words, the three horns that are "plucked out" represent the three kings that the Antichrist will conquer. In Daniel 11, we can understand who these three kings are.

Daniel 11:42–43, "He shall stretch out his hand against the countries, and the land of Egypt shall not escape. *He shall*

have power over the treasures of gold and silver, and over all the
precious things of Egypt; also the Libyans and Ethiopians shall
follow at his heels."

Daniel 11 is prophesying about the Antichrist, because the beginning of the paragraph in Daniel 11:40 uses the terminology, "at the time of the end," which is definitely pointing to the Antichrist's rule at the end of the age. If Daniel 7's fourth kingdom (beast) includes the rise of the little horn (Antichrist) from the ten kings, and he conquers three of the kings, then the fourth beast (kingdom) of Daniel 7 is the Antichrist's kingdom. As we journey forward, keep in mind that Daniel declared that the Antichrist's kingdom will consist of the iron metal component (Dan. 7:7).

DANIEL 7'S BEASTS

1. Lion- Babylonian Empire
2. Bear - Medo-Persian Empire
3. Leopard - Grecian Empire/ Four Regions of Grecian Empire
4. Iron - Antichrist's Kingdom/ Little Horn (Antichrist)

After Daniel concludes the vision of the four beasts, including the Antichrist's kingdom, the vision shifts to heaven!

Daniel 7:9–11, 13–14, "I watched till thrones were put in place, and the Ancient of Days was seated; His garment was white as snow, and the hair of His head was like pure wool. His throne was a fiery flame, its wheels a burning fire; A fiery stream issued and came forth from before Him. A thousand thousands ministered to Him; Ten thousand times ten thousand stood before Him. The court was seated, and the books were opened. I watched then because of the sound of the pompous words which the horn was speaking; I watched till the beast was slain, and its body destroyed and given to the burning flame. "I was watching in the night visions, and behold, One like the Son of Man, coming with the clouds of heaven! He came to the Ancient of Days, and they brought Him near before Him. Then to Him was given dominion and glory and a kingdom, that all peoples, nations, and languages should serve Him. His dominion is an everlasting dominion, which shall not pass away, and His kingdom the one which shall not be destroyed."

Daniel is definitely prophesying about God Almighty, His throne, judgment day, and Messiah, as the vision shifts to a heavenly scene. Daniel states, "His garment was white as snow, His hair was like pure wool, and His throne was like a fiery flame," which certainly describes the Lord. He portrays the throne in heaven as a place where "thousands ministered to Him and tens of thousands stood before Him in the court and the books were opened," referencing the Lord's judgment day. In the book of Revelation, John also describes a similar vision of the Ancient of Days, the Almighty.

Revelation 1:14, "His head and hair were white like wool, as white as snow, and His eyes like a flame of fire."

Revelation 5:11, "Then I looked, and I heard the voice of many angels around the throne, the living creatures, and the elders; and the number of them was ten thousand times ten thousand, and thousands of thousands."

Daniel 7 also gives us great insight into Messiah's Second Coming and millennial reign (1,000 years), as he describes "One like the Son of Man coming with the clouds of heaven" (Matt. 24:30). Daniel continues to explain that at Messiah's glorious appearing, the Antichrist will be slain and cast alive into the lake of fire, which is burning with brimstone (Rev. 19:20). He also confirms that the Ancient of Days (God) will give Messiah dominion, glory, and a *kingdom* that all nations and people will serve, which is the millennial kingdom. At Messiah's Second Coming and millennial reign (1,000 years), His kingdom will be everlasting, and it will continue into Eternity, the New Jerusalem! (Rev. 21–22).

Just as Daniel 8 is an end of the age prophecy, Daniel 7 is an end of the age prophecy, as well! In Daniel 7, Daniel describes the four major kingdoms that will rise to power, including the Antichrist's kingdom (fourth kingdom), and sequentially continues to describe a vision of God Almighty, Messiah, the Second Coming, and the millennial reign. Additionally, Daniel's prophecy of God, Messiah, and the Second Coming perfectly aligns with John's vision in Revelation, which is an end of the age prophecy. Although prophetic foreshadows of the first three kingdoms have occurred in history, Daniel 7 is a vision of sequential kingdoms and events that will occur at the end of the age.

DANIEL 7'S BEASTS AND EVENTS

1. Lion - Babylonian Empire
2. Bear - Medo-Persian Empire
3. Leopard - Grecian Empire/Four Regions of Grecian Empire
4. Iron - Antichrist's Kingdom/ Little Horn (Antichrist)
5. Messiah's Second Coming
6. Messiah's Millennial Reign (1,000-year reign on Earth)

It is important for us to understand that the events in Daniel 7 are in sequence, and will occur in the exact order which were prophesied after the 1948 and 1967 prophecies. As we discussed in Daniel 8, often times the prophets used prophetic foreshadows so that we can understand what events to expect in the future. Now, let us explore the interpretation of Daniel 7.

Daniel 7:16–18, "I came near to one of those who stood by, and asked him the truth of all this. So he told me and made known to me the interpretation of these things: 'Those great beasts, which are four, are four kings which arise out of the earth. But the saints of the Most High shall receive the kingdom, and possess the kingdom forever, even forever and ever.'"

The interpreter verifies that the four beasts of the vision are "four kings that will rise out of the earth, but the saints of the Most High will receive the kingdom and possess it forever and ever." Please note, the interpreter explains that there are only *four* kingdoms before Messiah's millennial kingdom, which include the Babylonian, Medo-Persian, Grecian, and Antichrist kingdoms. The kingdoms will come to power in the exact order of sequence followed by Messiah's millennial kingdom. After the interpreter tells Daniel about the four kings (beasts) that will rise out of the earth at the end of the age, Daniel inquires about the fourth beast and the little horn who made war against the saints until Messiah's Second Coming (Dan. 7:19–22).

Daniel 7:23–27, "Thus he said: 'The fourth beast shall be a fourth kingdom on earth, which shall be different from all other kingdoms, and shall devour the whole earth, trample it and break it in pieces. The ten horns are ten kings who shall arise from this kingdom. And another shall rise after them; He shall be different from the first ones, and shall subdue three kings. He shall speak pompous words against the Most High, shall persecute the saints of the Most High, and shall intend to change times and law. Then the saints shall be given into his hand for a time and times and half a time. 'But the court shall be seated, and they shall take away his dominion, to consume and destroy it forever. Then the kingdom and dominion, and the greatness of the kingdoms under the whole heaven, shall be given to the people, the saints of the Most High. His kingdom is an everlasting kingdom, and all dominions shall serve and obey Him.'"

The interpreter tells Daniel that the fourth kingdom (beast) will devour the whole earth, and it will consist of ten kings (horns). As we discovered, the fourth kingdom is the Antichrist's kingdom, because the Antichrist will rise to power after the ten kings and conquer three of them. The actions of the little horn, which include speaking pompous words against the Most High, persecuting the saints, and having authority for the last three and a half years of the age (Great Tribulation), clearly points to the Antichrist (Dan. 11:30-36, 12:7). Once the appointed time is completed, the courts shall be seated and the fourth kingdom's (Antichrist's) dominion will be destroyed, and Messiah's kingdom and dominion will rule forever and ever!

Certainly, the fourth kingdom is the Antichrist's kingdom, because it is the kingdom that will occur in sequence before Messiah's Second Coming and millennial reign. Daniel 7's description of the "little horn" also perfectly aligns with the characteristics of the Antichrist.

Just as in Daniel 8, Daniel 7 also describes a sequence of kingdoms that will rise to power, and then a "little horn" that will rise to prominence. So, if God's angel Gabriel emphatically proclaimed that Daniel 8 is a vision of the end, and it speaks of the "little horn" rising to power from the Grecian Empire (Seleucid region), and Daniel 7 speaks of the same little horn, then it also confirms that Daniel 7 is an end of the age prophecy, as well. These two visions and prophecies perfectly align with one another concerning the Medo-Persian, Grecian, and Antichrist kingdoms, which includes the Antichrist (little horn).

DANIEL 7'S BEASTS (KINGDOMS)

1. First Beast– Lion - Babylonian Empire (Iraq)

2. Second Beast – Bear - Medo-Persian Empire (Iran)
3. Third Beast – Leopard - Grecian Empire (Turkey)
4. Fourth Beast - Iron (Antichrist's Kingdom)

DANIEL 8'S BEASTS (KINGDOMS)

1. First Beast - Ram with two horns - Medo-Persia (Iran) correlates with Daniel 7's bear (Second beast)
2. Second Beast - Goat with one large horn - Grecian (Turkey) correlates with Daniel 7's leopard (third beast)
3. Third Beast - Little horn – Antichrist - (Turkey-Seleucid) correlates with Daniel 7's Fourth beast

CONCLUSION

Just as in Daniel 8, all of the kingdoms in Daniel 7 will also rise to power at the end of the age. Although Daniel 7 begins with the Babylonian Empire and Daniel 8 leads with the Medo-Persian Empire, the visions perfectly align with each other from the Medo-Persian Empire unto the Antichrist's kingdom. When we review the Medo-Persian and Grecian Empires of both visions, the prophecies present us with the same sequence of events that will occur after the 1948 and 1967 prophecies. Both prophecies explain that the Medo-Persian Empire will rise to power, then the Grecian Empire will follow, and it will be divided into four regions. After the four regions are established, the little horn (Antichrist) will rise from the Seleucid division of the Grecian Empire, and he will rule over the ten kings of the Antichrist's kingdom, which is the fourth and final beast before Messiah's Second Coming and millennial reign.

What about the Roman Empire? Are they not the people of the prince who is to come as prophesied in Daniel 9:26?

CHAPTER 4

THE PEOPLE OF THE PRINCE
WHO IS TO COME

One of the most beautiful prayers in the Holy Bible is found in Daniel 9. It is a prayer we can use to model our individual prayers, as well as our prayers for our nation. While Daniel was praying, the angel Gabriel appeared to him yet again. Gabriel gave Daniel a riddle for understanding the events of Messiah's First and Second Coming. We will not explore the mathematical aspect of the riddle, but instead, we will verify who "the people of the prince who is to come" actually are. This will confirm that the Roman Empire is not the prophesied people that Daniel is speaking about, as many people believe.

> Daniel 9:25–26, "And after the sixty-two weeks Messiah shall be cut off, but not for Himself; *And the people of the prince who is to come shall destroy the city and the sanctuary.*" (emphasis mine)

At first glance, it would be easy to conclude that since the Roman Empire (Titus) destroyed Jerusalem and the temple in AD 70, then Rome or Europe is where the Antichrist will rise from. However, when we take a more responsible approach and look deeper into this revelation, it becomes very clear that "the people of the prince who is to come" are not from Rome or Europe. Obviously, the Roman Empire did destroy Jerusalem and the temple, but who were the actual people that "formed" the division of the Roman Empire that destroyed the holy city? Once we understand who these people are, then we can confirm what area that "the people of the prince who is to come" are located, thus, verifying once again the region of the Antichrist.

Roman General Titus, who was in command of the destruction of Jerusalem and the temple, was also in charge of the Eastern division of the Roman Empire, which was primarily located in the Middle East. Publius Cornelius Tacitus, a well-respected historian and Roman Empire expert, chronicled the specific regions and "people" that comprised the legions that destroyed Jerusalem and the temple. He wrote, "Titus Caesar . . . found in Judaea three legions, the 5th, the 10th, and the 15th . . . To these he added the 12th from Syria, and some men belonging to the 18th and 3rd, whom he had withdrawn from Alexandria. This force was accompanied . . . by a strong contingent of *Arabs*, who hated the Jews with the usual hatred of neighbors..."[1]

Tacitus confirms that the "people" of the legions primarily consisted of Arabs, which included Syrians, Turks, and Egyptians (Alexandria). Here are the main legions of the Eastern division who destroyed Jerusalem and the temple:

1. Legion 3: Gallica - (Syria), Stationed in Syria
2. Legion 5: Macedonia - (Serbia, Bulgaria), Stationed in Judea
3. Legion 10: Fretensis - (Syria, Turkey), Stationed in Syria
4. Legion 12: Fulminata - (Syria, Turkey), Stationed in Asia Minor (Turkey) and Syria
5. Legion 15: Apollinaris - (Syria), Stationed in Syria
6. Legion 18: Egypt, Stationed in Egypt

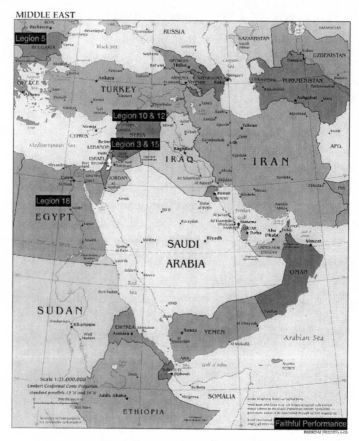

Roman Legions who destroyed Jerusalem

Flavius Josephus, a renowned Jewish historian, also recorded the following about General Titus' recruitment of the "people" in his legions. He wrote, "So Vespasian sent his son Titus [who], came by land into Syria, where he gathered together the Roman forces, with a considerable number of auxiliaries from the kings in that neighborhood."[2]

Historians Tacitus and Josephus both recorded that Titus' six legions of the eastern division of the Roman Empire were primarily made up of Syrians, Turks, Egyptians, and Arabs in general. As we journey forward, it is imperative to understand that these regions are all located in Islamic Muslim nations of today.

Josephus also recorded the following statements to confirm who the "people" are in Daniel's prophecy:

- The greatest part of the Roman garrison was raised out of Syria; and being thus related to the Syrian part, they were ready to assist."[3]

- "Malchus also, the king of Arabia, sent a thousand horsemen, besides five thousand footmen, the greatest part of which were archers; so that the whole army, including the auxiliaries send by the kings, as well as horsemen and footmen, when all were united together, amounted to sixty thousand."[4]

- "The multitude of the Arabians, with the Syrians, cut up those that came as suppliants, and searched their bellies. Nor does it seem to me that any misery befell the Jews that was more terrible than this, since in one night's time about two thousand of these deserters were thus infected." [5]

When we examine the six main legions under Titus that destroyed Jerusalem and the temple, the "people" certainly were not from Rome or Europe, but from the Middle Eastern areas of Syria, Turkey, Egypt, and other Arab nations.

1. Legion 3: Gallica - (Syria), Stationed in Syria
2. Legion 5: Macedonia - (Serbia, Bulgaria), Stationed in Judea
3. Legion 10: Fretensis - (Syria, Turkey), Stationed in Syria
4. Legion 12: Fulminata - (Syria, Turkey), Stationed in Asia Minor (Turkey) and Syria

5. Legion 15: Apollinaris - (Syria), Stationed in Syria
6. Legion 18: Egypt, Stationed in Egypt

These six legions were directly involved in the destruction of Jerusalem and the temple. Legion 10, the Fretensis Legion (Turkey/Syria), was the specific legion responsible for the destruction of the temple.[6]

Now, let us explore the Hebrew word for "the people of the prince" to give us final confirmation. In the *Hebrew Strong's Dictionary*, #5971, the word for "people of the prince" is *Am*. In English, it is translated, "a united or common people, tribes, or kinsmen." Surely, the Turks, Syrians, Egyptians, and Arabs of the Eastern division of the Roman Empire were not a "united common people or kinsmen" with the Romans or Europeans. Daniel clearly wrote this prophecy in a particular way in order for us to search and understand its true meaning.

CONCLUSION

It is important to understand that when Daniel prophesied about the kingdoms in the book of Daniel, he used symbolism of animals and metal components, but he did not use the word *people*. Also, throughout the Scriptures, Messiah and the prophets used the term *mountains* when speaking about kingdoms and empires, but they did not use the word *people* to describe them, as well. (Micah 4; Matt. 17; Rev. 17). Certainly, Daniel wrote the prophecy, "the people of the prince who is to come" in a different way than when he prophesied about a kingdom. "The people of the prince who is to come" are not from Europe or the Roman Empire, but from the Middle Eastern areas of Turkey, Iraq, and Syria, which are today Islamic Muslim nations.

CHAPTER 5

NEBUCHADNEZZAR'S
STATUE DREAM

N ow that we understand that God's prophetic timeline of Messiah's Second Coming was "activated" with the fulfillment of the 1948 and 1967 prophecies, that Daniel 7 and 8 are end of the age prophecies that will occur from those divinatory years, and have knowledge of who are "the people of the prince who is to come," let us explore Daniel 2. Is Daniel 2 an end of the age prophecy that perfectly aligns with Daniel 7 and Daniel 8 in their respective kingdoms?

The prophecy of Daniel 2, Nebuchadnezzar's famous statue dream, occurred in the second year of his reign over Babylon in approximately 604 BC (Dan. 2:1). During this time, Nebuchadnezzar had a dream that troubled him and he could not sleep (Dan. 2:1). He called the wise men of Babylon, including the magicians, astrologers, sorcerers, and Chaldeans, to explain the dream and its interpretation to him (Dan. 2:2–3). However, instead of telling Nebuchadnezzar what the dream was before they told him its interpretation, as he had asked them to do, the wise men asked him to describe the dream to them before they would reveal the meaning of it (Dan. 2:4).

Nevertheless, Nebuchadnezzar was firm in his decision not to explain the dream to them (Dan. 2:5–9). The wise men told Nebuchadnezzar that his request to interpret the dream was impossible for any man to reveal without him first telling them what the dream was about. Furious, Nebuchadnezzar gave the command to destroy all of the wise men of Babylon, including Daniel and his friends (Dan. 2:10–13). Once Daniel heard of the king's command, he and his friends petitioned God to help them understand the dream, and the Almighty blessed Daniel with the knowledge of the dream and its interpretation (Dan. 2:17–19). After Daniel praised God for His love, mercy, and grace (Dan. 2:20–25), he revealed to Nebuchadnezzar the dream and its interpretation (Dan. 2:20–25).

> Daniel 2:27–29, "Daniel answered in the presence of the king, and said, "The secret which the king has demanded, the wise men, the astrologers, the magicians, and the soothsayers cannot declare to the king. But there is a God in heaven who reveals secrets, and He has made known to King Nebuchadnezzar what will be in the *latter days*. Your dream, and the visions of your head upon your bed, were these: As for you, O king, thoughts came to your mind while on your bed, about what would come to pass after this; and He who reveals secrets has made known to you what will be."

Daniel 2 is one of the most interesting yet debated prophecies in the Holy Bible. Some believe that this prophecy has mostly been fulfilled in ancient history, with the remaining fulfillments to occur at the end of the age and Messiah's Second Coming. However, Daniel clearly states at the beginning of this prophecy that its interpretation is for the "latter days" (Dan. 2:28), which is an eschatological term for the end of the age. In other words, we can understand this to indicate that every kingdom and event of Daniel 2 will occur at the end of the age and conclude at Messiah's Second Coming and millennial reign. Now, let us discover this incredible prophecy as Daniel explains the dream to Nebuchadnezzar.

Daniel 2:31–35, "You, O king, were watching; and behold, a great image! This great image, whose splendor was excellent, stood before you; and its form was awesome. This image's head was of fine gold, its chest and arms of silver, its belly and thighs of bronze, its legs of iron, its feet partly of iron and partly of clay. You watched while a stone was cut out without hands, which struck the image on its feet of iron and clay, and broke them in pieces. Then the iron, the clay, the bronze, the silver, and the gold were *crushed together,* and became like chaff from the summer threshing floors; the wind carried them away so that no trace of them was found. And the stone that struck the image became a great mountain and filled the whole earth."

Daniel describes the statue as a great image with metal components for each of its major body parts. After a head-to-toe description of the metal components to the body parts, he states that a stone cut without hands struck the image on its feet of iron and clay and broke them into pieces. It is very important to understand that once the stone struck the image on its feet, *all* of the metal components were *crushed together,* meaning the stone will conquer and destroy all of the metal components at *one* time. Daniel concludes the vision of the dream by stating, "the stone that struck the image became a great mountain and filled the whole earth." As we discussed earlier, mountains are symbolic for kingdoms, since stones cannot fill the earth, but kingdoms can fill the earth. Now, let us discover the interpretation of this prophecy.

Daniel 2:36–38, "This is the dream. Now we will tell the interpretation of it before the king. You, O king, are a king of kings. For the God of heaven has given you a kingdom, power, strength, and glory; and wherever the children of men dwell, or the beasts of the field and the birds of the heaven,

He has given them into your hand, and has made you ruler over them all—*you are this head of gold.*" (emphasis mine)

Daniel begins the interpretation of the dream by prophesying that the Babylonian Empire is the component of gold. Remember, Daniel definitively proclaimed that this prophecy was for the "latter days," which is the end of the age. Please note, Nebuchadnezzar ruled Babylon from 606–562 BC, so clearly that was not the end of the age. When Daniel told Nebuchadnezzar, "you are this head of gold," he was implying that the Babylonian Empire is the metal component, not Nebuchadnezzar himself.

Daniel 2:39–40, "But after you shall arise another kingdom inferior to yours; then another, a third kingdom of bronze, which shall rule over all the earth. And the fourth kingdom shall be as strong as iron, inasmuch as iron breaks in pieces and shatters everything; and like iron that crushes, that kingdom will break in pieces and crush all the others."

Daniel continues to explain to Nebuchadnezzar that a second kingdom will rise after the Babylonian Empire, then a third kingdom, and a fourth. Most Bible scholars and prophecy teachers agree that the first three kingdoms are Babylonian (gold), Medo-Persian (silver), and Grecian (bronze), as they rule the Earth in the exact sequence in history. As we move forward, keep in mind that Daniel states that only *four* kingdoms rise to power, just as Daniel 7 prophesied. Here are the first three kingdoms of Daniel 2. Who is the fourth kingdom, which is the metal component of iron?

DANIEL 2'S STATUE

1. Gold - Babylonian Empire
2. Silver - Medo-Persian Empire
3. Bronze - Grecian Empire
4. Iron?

Daniel 2 describes the fourth kingdom as the metal component of iron (Dan. 2:40) that will crush *all* of the other kingdoms before

it. This implies that the fourth kingdom will also conquer all of the land area that the previous kingdoms controlled, as well. It is a widely held view that the fourth kingdom is the Roman Empire, because it followed the Grecian Empire as the ancient world power, and it also seems to correlate with the two legs of the statue (Eastern and Western division of the Roman Empire). However, this theory is not biblically or historically accurate, because according to Daniel, the fourth empire crushes *all* of the other empires before it, and also the respective land areas (Daniel 2:40).

Nebuchadnezzar's Statue

Did the Roman Empire "crush" the Medo-Persian Empire? During the dominance of the Roman Empire, the Parthians (Persians) controlled the region of land east of the Euphrates River (Iraq). As history proves, the Roman Empire did not "crush" all of the Medo-Persian Empire, because it never conquered Parthia (Persia).[1] Justin's *History of the World* recorded this statement about the Parthian's wars against the Romans: "The Parthians, in whose hands the empire of the east now is, having divided the world, as it were, with the Romans, were originally exiles from Scythia . . . Being assailed by the Romans, also, in three wars, under the conduct of the greatest generals, and at the most flourishing period of the republic, they alone, of all nations, were not only a match for them, but came off victorious."[2] Below is a map that outlines the Roman Empire's conquered territory at the pinnacle of its dominance.

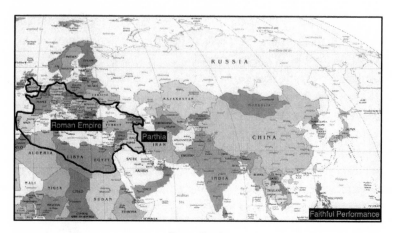

Roman Empire

As we can see, the Roman Empire never conquered Parthia (Medo-Persian Empire), thus eliminating it from becoming the fourth kingdom of Daniel's prophecy. On the contrary, the Medo-Persian Empire conquered all of the Babylonian Empire, and the Grecian Empire conquered all of the Babylonian and the Medo-Persian Empire, just as Daniel prophesied.

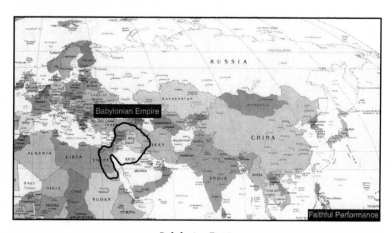

Babylonian Empire

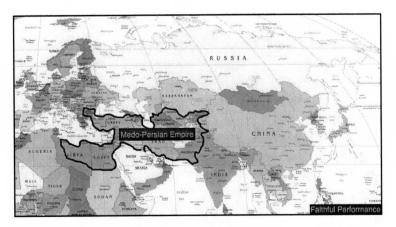

Medo-Persian Empire

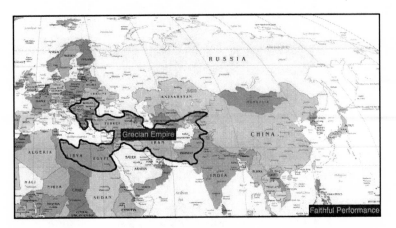

Grecian Empire

Remember, Daniel prophesied that these kingdoms will occur in the "latter days," so these empires were prophetic foreshadows that give us wisdom and knowledge of what will ultimately occur at the end of the age (latter days).

Just as we discovered that the Roman Empire is not the fourth kingdom of Daniel 7, it is also not the fourth kingdom of Daniel 2, since the Romans did not conquer all of the land area of the previous empires (Parthia). In summary, let us review Daniel 7's first three kingdoms (beasts) and compare them to Daniel 2's first three kingdoms (metal components).

Nebuchadnezzar's Statue Dream

DANIEL 2

1. Babylonian Empire (Gold)
2. Medo-Persian Empire (Silver)
3. Grecian Empire (Bronze)

DANIEL 7

1. Babylonian Empire (Lion)
2. Medo-Persian Empire (Bear)
3. Grecian Empire (Leopard)

The first three beasts (kingdoms) of Daniel 7 are exactly the same as the first three metal components (kingdoms) of Daniel 2! Both prophecies perfectly coincide with one another and also occur in the exact sequence. Now, let us discover the fourth kingdom of Daniel 2 in order to see if it matches Daniel 7's fourth kingdom.

> Daniel 2:40, "And the fourth kingdom shall be as strong as *iron,* inasmuch as iron breaks in pieces and shatters everything; and like *iron* that crushes, that kingdom will break in pieces and *crush all the others.*"

> Daniel 7:7, "A fourth beast, dreadful and terrible, exceedingly strong. It had huge *iron* teeth; it was devouring, breaking in pieces, and trampling the residue with its feet."

Daniel is telling us that the fourth kingdom in both Daniel 2 and Daniel 7 are the same kingdom (iron), just as the other three kingdoms are identical. If Daniel 7's fourth kingdom, which is represented by iron, is the Antichrist's kingdom, then the fourth kingdom in Daniel 2, which is also represented by iron, is the Antichrist's kingdom, as well.

DANIEL 2 - STATUE DREAM

1. Babylonian Empire (Gold)
2. Medo-Persian Empire (Silver)
3. Grecian Empire (Bronze)
4. Antichrist's Kingdom (Iron)

DANIEL 7 - FOUR KINGDOMS

1. Babylonian Empire (Lion)
2. Medo-Persian Empire (Bear)
3. Grecian Empire (Leopard)
4. Antichrist's Kingdom (Iron)

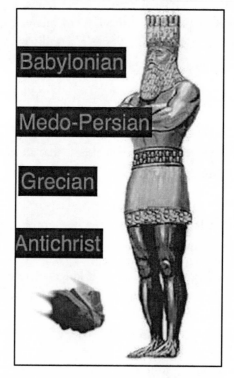

Nebuchadnezzar's Statue Dream

Daniel 2 and Daniel 7 perfectly align with each other, because the four empires are in unified succession in both prophecies: Babylonian, Medo-Persian, Grecian, and the Antichrist's kingdom. Furthermore, Daniel 8 also confirms Daniel 2 and Daniel 7!

DANIEL 2

1. Babylonian Empire (Gold) (Dan. 2:38)
2. Medo-Persian Empire (Silver) (Dan. 8:20–21)
3. Grecian Empire (Bronze) (Dan. 8:20–21)
4. Antichrist's Kingdom (Iron) (Daniel 2:40; 7:7, 19)

DANIEL 7

1. Babylonian Empire (Lion) (Dan. 2:38)
2. Medo-Persian Empire (Bear) (Dan. 8:20–21)
3. Grecian Empire (Leopard) (Dan. 8:20–21)
4. Antichrist's Kingdom (Iron) (Daniel 2:40; 7:7, 19)

DANIEL 8

1. Medo-Persian Empire (ram) - Coincides with Daniel 2 & Daniel 7's second beast (Dan. 8:20-21)
2. Grecian Empire (goat)- Coincides with Daniel 2 & Daniel 7's third beast (Dan. 8:20-21)
3. The Antichrist's kingdom (little horn) - Coincides with Daniel 2 & Daniel 7's fourth beast

Daniel 8 begins with the Medo-Persian Empire, not the Babylonian Empire. However, as we can see, the Medo-Persian and Grecian Empires of Daniel 8 perfectly coincide with Daniel 2 and Daniel 7's respective kingdoms. Most Bible scholars and prophecy teachers agree that the first three kingdoms in Daniel 2 and Daniel 7 are the Babylonian, Medo-Persian, and Grecian Empires. In fact, Daniel confirms who the first three kingdoms (beasts) are in his prophecies, as well: Babylonian Empire (Dan. 2:38), Medo-Persian and Grecian Empire (Dan. 8:20–21).

Daniel 8 concludes by describing in detail how the Grecian Empire divides into four smaller regions before the reign of the fourth kingdom, the Antichrist's kingdom. However, this does not take away from the continuing sequence of the four kingdoms that occur in Daniel 2 and Daniel 7. In fact, it embellishes all of the prophecies, because it gives more detail into what region the Antichrist will rise from, which is the Seleucid division of the Grecian Empire.

GOD'S PROPHETIC TIMELINE:

1. 1948 Prophecy
2. 1967 Prophecy
3. Babylonian Empire
4. Medo-Persian Empire
5. Grecian Empire > Four smaller regions > 10 Kings > Antichrist will rise (Seleucid division)
6. Antichrist's Kingdom = seven-year tribulation
7. Messiah's Second Coming
8. Messiah's Millennial Reign
9. New Jerusalem

Before we continue, it is imperative to understand that all of the kingdoms that are prophesied in Daniel 2, 7, and 8 are Islamic Muslim nations; Babylonian (Iraq), Medo-Persian (Kurds-Iran), and Grecian (Turkey). To be clear, this is not to say that all of the Arab people living in these areas are Islamic Muslims, because there are hundreds of thousands of Arab believers in Messiah (Isaiah 17 and 19; Acts 15:17). Hallelujah! With that being said, we can be confident that the Antichrist's kingdom (fourth kingdom) will also consist of Islamic Muslim nations as we will discover in a later chapter. What about the feet and toes of the statue?

Daniel 2:41–43, "Whereas you saw the feet and toes, partly of potter's clay and partly of iron, *the kingdom* shall be divided; yet the strength of the iron shall be in it, just as you saw the iron mixed with ceramic clay. And as the toes of the feet were partly of iron and partly of clay, so the kingdom shall be partly strong and partly fragile. As you saw iron mixed with ceramic clay, they will mingle with the seed of men; but they will not adhere to one another, just as iron does not mix with clay."

Daniel continues the interpretation of the *fourth kingdom, the Antichrist's kingdom,* by describing the feet and ten toes of the statue, which symbolize the ten kings *of* the Antichrist's kingdom. Daniel confirms that the feet and ten toes are a continuation of the fourth kingdom by declaring, "whereas you saw the feet and toes, partly of potter's clay and partly of iron, *the kingdom* (fourth kingdom) shall be divided."

Daniel never proclaimed or prophesied about a fifth kingdom, but stated "the kingdom," continuing his description of the fourth kingdom, which is the Antichrist's kingdom (Daniel 2:41). Daniel is giving us a deeper insight into the "make-up" of the Antichrist's kingdom.

The ten toes represent the ten kings of the Antichrist's kingdom (iron), as they are connected to the legs of iron (Antichrist's kingdom). Daniel prophesies that the Antichrist's kingdom will be divided (iron and clay), which refers to the two major divisions of Islam, the Sunnis and the Shiites. We can understand the two different sects of Islam as Medo-Persian-Iran (Shiite) and Grecian-Turkey (Sunni). Daniel declares that one of the divisions will be stronger (iron) than the other (clay), which confirms the prophecies of Daniel 2, 7, and 8, because the Grecian Empire (Sunnis) will conquer the Medo-Persian Empire (Shiite) (Dan. 8:6–7). The Sunnis will be the iron (strong) and the Shias will be the clay. Ezekiel 38-39 also confirms this, as the Antichrist (Gog) will rise from Turkey (Sunni), the land of Magog, and will be joined by Iran (Persia), but Turkey (Sunni) will be the leader of the alliance. At the end of the age, these two sects of Islam, Sunni and Shiite, will become of "one mind," coming together for the common purpose of destroying Israel and fighting Messiah at His Second Coming.

> Revelation 17:12–14, "The ten horns which you saw are *ten kings* who have received no kingdom as yet, but they receive authority for one hour as kings with the beast. *These are of one mind, and they will give their power and authority to the beast. These will make war with the Lamb, and the Lamb will overcome them, for He is Lord of lords and King of kings; and those who are with Him are called, chosen, and faithful."* (Also see Ezek. 38:1–6)

Daniel concludes the interpretation of the statute:

> Daniel 2:34–35, "You watched while a stone was cut out without hands, which struck the image on its feet of iron and clay, and broke them in pieces. Then the iron, the clay, the bronze, the silver, and the gold were *crushed together*, and became like chaff from the summer threshing floors; the wind carried them away so that no trace of them was found. And the stone that struck the image became a great mountain and filled the whole earth."

Daniel prophesies that Messiah, "the stone cut without hands," will crush *all* of the previous four empires at His Second Coming, which are the Babylonian (gold), Medo-Persian (silver), Grecian (bronze), and Antichrist kingdoms (iron), including the ten kings (iron and clay). Daniel is telling us that all of these empires will rise at the end of the age before Messiah's Second Coming, and Messiah will crush *all* of them together. Then, Messiah's kingdom will be an everlasting kingdom (mountain) and will stand forever! Hallelujah!

Daniel 2:44–45, *"And in the days of these kings* the God of heaven will set up a kingdom which shall never be destroyed; and the kingdom shall not be left to other people; it shall break in pieces and consume all these kingdoms, and it shall stand forever."

Daniel prophesies that *"in the days of these kings,"* the God of heaven will set up a Kingdom that shall never be destroyed, which will consume *all* of the kingdoms in Daniel 2. Daniel is prophesying about Messiah's millennial kingdom, and he confirms that all of the kingdoms prophesied in Daniel 2 (in the days of these kings) will rise to power at the end of the age (latter days) before Messiah's Second Coming.

CONCLUSION

Daniel 2 is an end of the age prophecy just like Daniel 7 and Daniel 8. Daniel confirms this by proclaiming that Daniel 2 will be fulfilled in the "latter days" (Daniel 2:28), and also that Messiah will set up His everlasting kingdom (Second Coming and millennial reign) during the "days of these kings" (Daniel 2:44). Also, in Daniel 12, Daniel is told to seal up his book until the time of the end (Daniel 12:4), also confirming that the visions and prophecies of Daniel 2, 7, and 8, are for the end of the age. As we discovered, Daniel 2, 7, and 8, perfectly align with each other according to the kingdoms in each prophecy. The question is, "What kingdom is our generation living in today?"

CHAPTER 6

WHAT KINGDOM IS
OUR GENERATION LIVING IN TODAY?

If the prophetic fulfillments of the 1948 and 1967 prophecies accelerated God's prophetic timeline for Messiah's Second Coming, have the kingdoms of Daniel 2, 7, and 8 begun to reach their fulfillment? If so, what kingdom are we living in today, and what events can we expect to occur in the future? As we continue on God's prophetic timeline, let us begin with the first prophesied kingdom, the Babylonian Empire.

GOD'S PROPHETIC TIMELINE:

1. 1948 Prophecy
2. 1967 Prophecy
3. Babylonian Empire
4. Medo-Persian Empire
5. Grecian Empire > Four smaller regions > Ten Kings > Antichrist will rise (Seleucid division)
6. Antichrist's Empire (ten kings) = seven-year tribulation
7. Messiah's Second Coming
8. Messiah's Millennial Reign
9. New Jerusalem

THE FIRST KINGDOM-THE BABYLONIAN EMPIRE

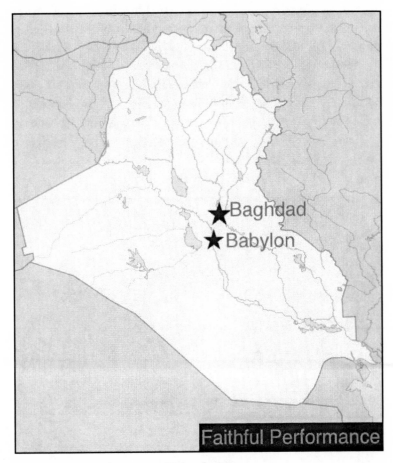

Modern day Iraq

According to Daniel 2 and Daniel 7, the first kingdom that will rise to power at the end of the age is the Babylonian Empire. Today, we have enough biblical and historical information to substantiate that Iraq is the kingdom Daniel is referring to, because ancient Babylon, the capital of the Babylonian Empire, was located within the borders of modern-day Iraq. In fact, in the 1980s, Saddam Hussein began to rebuild the ancient ruins of the pagan city with the ultimate goal of recreating ancient Babylon. He invested hundreds of millions of dollars into new construction for the restoration of the Babylonian Empire's historical monuments and artifacts.[1]

Saddam idolized Nebuchadnezzar with such reverence that as he restored the ancient buildings and artifacts, his name was inscribed on over 60 million bricks in order to imitate and pay homage to Nebuchadnezzar. One inscription read: "This was built by Saddam Hussein, son of Nebuchadnezzar, to glorify Iraq."[2] Another inscription read, "In the era of Saddam Hussein, the protector of Iraq, who rebuilt civilization and rebuilt Babylon."[3]

Bricks-CPhoto Credit AP/Karim Kadim

Saddam also installed a portrait of Nebuchadnezzar and himself at the entrance to the ancient ruins, and he reestablished the "*Lion of Babylon,*" which was a black rock sculpture dated about 2,600 years old. Remember, the lion refers to the animal that symbolically represents the Babylonian Empire in Daniel 7 and Revelation 13. From these few details, we can certainly see that Saddam Hussein wanted to emulate Nebuchadnezzar and "revive and restore" the Babylonian Empire (lion).

Furthermore, just as Nebuchadnezzar conquered Jerusalem (586 BC), Saddam had the same ambition, so that he could be like his "father." On January 18, 1991 (Gulf War), Iraqi scud missiles hit Tel Aviv, Israel.[4] During the war, Saddam made an infamous quote concerning the battle, stating, "The great duel, the mother of all battles has begun. The dawn of victory nears as this great showdown begins."[5] Over the course of the Gulf War, approximately thirty-nine scud missiles were fired at Israel. Eventually, the United States and its allies intervened on Saddam's blood-thirsty quest of the first Gulf War (1990-1991), and tensions settled in the Middle East for a period of time.

However, after the September 11th attacks on the World Trade Center in 2001, the United States and its allies fulfilled Biblical prophecy in 2003, when they removed Saddam Hussein and the Babylonian Empire (Iraq) from power over the Middle East. Just as the ancient Babylonian Empire was numbered, weighed in the balance, and found wanting by God (*Mene, Mene, Tekel, Upharsin,* Daniel 5), so was Saddam Hussein and the prophetic Babylonian Empire in 2003. This fulfilled the first kingdom's demise in the "latter days" found in Daniel 2 and Daniel 7 concerning God's prophetic timeline.

DANIEL 2

1. Babylonian Empire (Iraq)-Fulfilled
2. Medo-Persian Empire (Iran)
3. Grecian Empire (Turkey)
4. Antichrist's Kingdom

DANIEL 7

1. Babylonian Empire (Iraq)-Fulfilled
2. Medo-Persian Empire (Iran)
3. Grecian Empire (Turkey)
4. Antichrist's Kingdom

DANIEL 8

1. Medo-Persian Empire (Iran) - Coincides with Daniel 2 & Daniel 7's second beast
2. Grecian Empire (Turkey) - Coincides with Daniel 2 & Daniel 7's third beast
3. The Antichrist (little horn) - Coincides with Daniel 2 & Daniel 7's fourth beast

THE SECOND KINGDOM-THE MEDO-PERSIAN EMPIRE

What about the second prophesied kingdom, the Medo-Persian Empire (Iran)? After Saddam Hussein was removed from power in Iraq (2003), it did not take long before Iran (Medo-Persian Empire) began its march "westward, northward, and southward," just as Daniel 8:4 prophesied. As of today, Iran controls more than one-half of Iraq. Iran is also in direct control of Hezbollah (Lebanon), as they finance the terror group and supply them with weapons. Additionally, after Yemen President Ali Abdullah Saleh, an ally of Saudi Arabia, stepped down as president in 2011, Iran invaded Yemen, and they currently have influence and control over much of the country. This is a major development, because Yemen is located on Saudi Arabia's southern border and poses a national security risk. From a biblical standpoint this is profound, because the prophet Isaiah tells us that Iran (Medo-Persia) will destroy Saudi Arabia at the end of the age (Isa. 21).

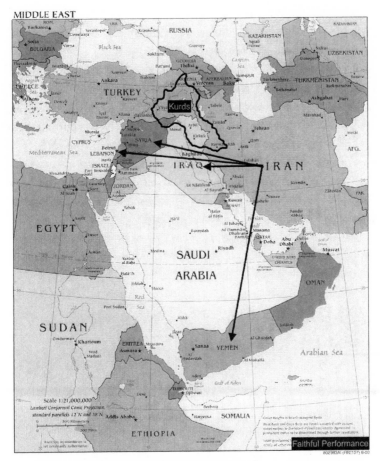

The Medo-Persian (Iran) March

In its most recent "march," Iran has ground troops in Syria, where, as of this writing, a civil war is at its climatic pinnacle. It is believed that Iran supports the Assad regime in Syria; however, this eventually could be the strategic location of the next great war in the Middle East, which we will discuss later in this chapter. To finalize Iran's military and financial dominance in the Middle East, the United States agreed to a catastrophic nuclear deal with the

Iranian dictatorship, which included a payment to them in the amount of $150 billion dollars. In August of 2016, the United States made another disastrous decision in making a $400 million cash payment for the hostages in Iran, although they deny this is a ransom payment. However, as of September 2016, it has been reported that the United States sent $1.7 billion for the hostages, which is four times the original amount! All of these events confirm Daniel 8's prophecy that *the ram (Iran) did according to his will and became great* (Daniel 8:4). Without any doubt, it is very clear that Iran (Medo-Persia) is the superpower of the Middle East as it "marches" across the land, confirming the sequence of kingdoms in Daniel 2, 7 and 8.

As of 2016, our generation, the terminal generation, is living in and witnessing the dominance of the Medo-Persian Empire (Iran) of Daniel 2, 7, and 8!

GOD'S PROPHETIC TIMELINE:

1948/1967 Prophecies- Fulfilled

DANIEL 2

1. Babylonian Empire (Iraq)-Fulfilled
2. Medo-Persian Empire (Iran) > 2016
3. Grecian Empire (Turkey)
4. Antichrist's Kingdom

DANIEL 7

1. Babylonian Empire (Iraq)-Fulfilled
2. Medo-Persian Empire (Iran) > 2016
3. Grecian Empire (Turkey)
4. Antichrist's Kingdom

WHAT KINGDOM IS OUR GENERATION LIVING IN TODAY?

DANIEL 8

1. Medo-Persian Empire (Iran) - Coincides with Daniel 2 and Daniel 7's second beast > 2016
2. Grecian Empire (Turkey) - Coincides with Daniel 2 and Daniel 7's third beast
3. The Antichrist (little horn)- Coincides with Daniel 2 and Daniel 7's fourth beast

THE STATUS OF AYATOLLAH KHAMENEI OF IRAN (PERSIA)

It is important to understand the status and health of the Iranian dictator, Ayatollah Ali Khamenei. The Second Supreme leader was a key figure and played a significant role in the 1979 Iranian Revolution with the First Supreme Leader, Sayyid Ruhollah Mūsavi Khomeini. Khamenei served as President under Khomeini from 1981–1989, and once Khomeini passed away in 1989, Khamenei became the Supreme leader of Iran from 1989 unto today. However, as of recent years, Khamenei is in declining health at the age of seventy-seven. On September 9, 2014, Khamenei underwent surgery for a "routine operation, as reported by Iran's controlled media.[6,7] Nevertheless, according to a report by *Le Figaro*, intelligence officials reported that he has prostate cancer. The report continued to reveal that "the cancer is in stage four, in other words it has spread." The doctors estimate Khamenei has "two years to live." [8, 9]

Certainly, Khamenei's health is very important to Iran's dominance over the Middle East, because he is one of only two supreme leaders of Iran since the Iranian Revolution of 1979 (Ruhollah Khomeini (1902–1989). *Forbes* listed the current Ayatollah in the top twenty-five of the world's most powerful people, so this fact cannot be overstated.[10] In the coming years, Khamenei's health will definitely figure into the dominance of the Medo-Persian (Iran) Empire over the Middle East.

THE NEXT GREAT WAR

Before we continue to explore the third prophesied kingdom, the Grecian Empire (Turkey), let us discover the next major event in Daniel's prophecies, which is the next great war of Daniel 8. According to Daniel, as the ram (Iran) becomes great, a male goat (Turkey) will rise to power, and he will attack the ram (Iran), "running at him with furious power, confronting him, and raging against him." Daniel prophesies that Turkey (goat) will win the next great war, as "it will break the two horned ram (Iran), cast him down to the ground and trample him, and the male goat (Turkey) will become very great." (Daniel 8:7-8)

So the question is, "has Turkey risen to power to begin its prophetic calling in Daniel 8?

THE THIRD KINGDOM - THE GRECIAN EMPIRE (TURKEY)

On July 24, 1923, the Republic of Turkey gained its democratic sovereignty, ending over 600 years of dictatorship from the Ottoman Empire (Treaty of Lausanne). The Republic was officially proclaimed on October 29, 1923, in the new capital of Ankara. Now, let us fast forward approximately eighty years to 2001 with the founding and establishment of the AKP party and the rise of its Prime Minister (2003–2014) and current President Recep Tayyip Erdogan (2014). Since the founding of the AKP party in the early 2000s, Turkey has been revolutionized into the fundamentalist Islamic ways of the old tyrannical Ottoman Empire dictatorship.

In 2013, after anti-government protests were held in Turkey by the Republican People's party, the opposition party to the AKP, then Prime Minister Erdogan alleged that over 1,863 journalists should lose their jobs because of their anti-government views.[11, 12, 13] During the 2013 protests, notable cases of media censorship also occurred because the mainstream media did not broadcast the demonstrations until after the fact.[14]

In 2014, Erdogan signed a bill into law allowing the government to block websites without a court order, thereby tightening his control over the internet.[15] The AKP party also blocked social media sites such as YouTube and Twitter after a recorded conversation between Erdogan and his son was released.[16] The infamous conversation allegedly portrays Erdogan warning his family to nullify all cash reserves amid the $100 billion government corruption scandal (2013).[17, 18]

In Erdogan's pompous anger to counter the embarrassment and humiliation over the private social media releases, he made a speech promising to "rip out the roots of Twitter," showing his frustration over the scandal.[19] Within hours, BTK regulators blocked DNS service to the site. However, the block of Twitter proved ineffective, because traffic to the site increased by a record of 138 percent![20] Two months later, the Constitutional Court ordered the ban to be lifted.[21] On March 11, 2016, in defiance and in an effort to intimidate the Constitutional Court's order, Erdogan stated in a live televised speech, "I hope the Constitutional Court would not again attempt such ways which will open its existence and legitimacy up for debate."[22]

In 2014, Erdogan's dictatorship declared war on the remaining free press in Turkey. He and his party passed a bill that allows the government the authority to block internet sites subject to court reviews within three days and granting it access to Internet traffic data.[23] These and many other instances underline the fact that Erdogan is swiftly moving Turkey into the fundamentalist ways of the old Ottoman Empire dictatorship and priming its prophetic calling in Daniel's prophecies.

Furthermore, Erdogan and the AKP party's relationship with Israel has been strained, to say the least. In 2010, after the Gaza flotilla raid, Erdogan condemned Israel's raid by calling it "state terrorism"; therefore, proclaiming Israel as "the main threat to regional peace."[24] He also accused Israel of transforming Gaza into an "open-air prison" and suggested that Israel's nuclear facilities come under

IAEA inspection.[25] In March 2012, during the Israeli-Gaza conflict, Erdogan stated that Israel needs to stop the "massacre and genocide" of the Palestinians in Gaza.[26] In August 2014, during another Israeli-Gaza war, Erdogan accused Israel of deliberately killing Palestinian women and mothers. He said, "They kill women so that they will not give birth to Palestinians; they kill babies so that they won't grow up; they kill men so they can't defend their country." Erdogan went on to proclaim, "Israel will drown in the blood they shed."[27] He even compared Israel to the infamous murderer Adolf Hitler by stating that Israel is "more barbaric than Hitler," and "Just like Hitler who sought to establish a race free of all faults, Israel is chasing after the same target."[28] However, being the hypocrite that he is, when asked at a press conference if he believed a presidential system was possible in a unitary state, Erdogan confirmed and referenced Nazi Germany as the prime example of how this would be possible!

In July of 2016, after a failed military coup attempt to overthrow Erdogan's dictatorship in Turkey, Erdogan has proven once again that his ultimate goal for the Turkish people and surrounding nations is to have a revived tyrannical Ottoman Empire dictatorship. Since the failed coup, approximately 20,000 plotters, 20,000 teachers, 10,000 police officers, 115 generals and admirals, 15,000 soldiers, 3,000 judges (1/3 of all judges in Turkey), including government officials have been investigated, interrogated, jailed, and/or released from their duties. Erdogan has also closed hundreds of schools for not being sufficiently Islamic (Shariah Law), and he also closed down 130 media outlets. Please note, this occurred in one month![30]

Now, let us discuss the most obvious and compelling evidence that Erdogan and the Grecian Empire (Turkey) is rising to power to challenge the Medo-Persian (Iran) Empire. In December of 2015, King Salman bin Abdulaziz of Saudi Arabia approved Turkish president Erdogan to enter the gates of the Kaaba (Bab-Illah) in Mecca, Saudi Arabia, to worship and pray to Allah.[29] As the Gate and Tower of Bab-Illah (Kaaba) is very sacred in Islam, this is only allowed for someone whom they feel is "godly." The CNN network reported some Egyptians saying, "We consider him as the Islamic leader in the Middle East."[31] Erdogan's "anointing" by Saudi Arabia, one of the most influential and wealthiest countries of the world is quite alarming, because it aligns Turkey and Saudi Arabia as allies. As Turkey (Grecian Empire) rises to power in the region to conquer Iran (Medo-Persia), their alliance cannot be overstated.

Please note, Iran (Shiite) and Saudi Arabia (Sunni) are enemies, because Iran believes that Saudi Arabia is a blasphemy to Islam because of their civility towards Israel and the West. Furthermore, the deep hatred between the two countries results from a theological difference in the separate approaches to Islam (Shiite and Sunni).

In fact, in September of 2016, Saudi Grand Mufti Al-Sheikh Abdulaziz remarked that the Iranian leaders "are not Muslim."[32] In response to Abdulaziz's verbal defamation, the Iranians said, "Indeed; no resemblance between Islam of Iranians and most Muslims and bigoted extremism that Wahhabi (Saudi Arabia) top cleric and Saudi terror masters preach."[33]

The war of words between the two enemies have escalated since January of 2016, when Saudi Arabia beheaded Sheikh Nimr Baqir al-Nimr, a prominent Shiite Muslim cleric and dissident.[34] Iranian Ayatollah Ahmad Khatami strongly condemned this act and said, "If Sheikh Nimr is executed, Saudi Arabia should be ready for dire consequences and will pay a heavy price."[35] In response, the Saudi embassy in Iran was attacked and burned.[36] These recent events have compounded and deepened the hatred between the two countries. The interesting twist is that according to the Biblical prophets, Turkey will conquer Iran (Dan. 2, 7, 8), and Iran will eventually destroy Saudi Arabia (Isa. 21), as we journey toward the end of the age to Messiah's Second Coming. Certainly, the "anointing" of Erdogan at the Kaaba in Mecca is very important and cannot be overstated.

Furthermore, in February of 2016, as the Syrian war reached its pinnacle, a military operation in Saudi Arabia called "North Thunder" formed as an opposition to Iran's land ambitions across the Middle East, including Syria. "North Thunder" consists of twenty

Arab and Muslim countries and the GCC-formed Peninsula Shield led by Saudi Arabia. The twenty countries are: Saudi Arabia, the UAE, Jordan, Bahrain, Senegal, Sudan, Kuwait, Maldives, Morocco, Pakistan, Chad, Tunis, Djibouti, Comoros, Oman, Qatar, Malaysia, Egypt, Mauritania, and Mauritius.[37] North Thunder consists of approximately 150,000 soldiers, 2,540 warplanes, 20,000 tanks, and 460 helicopters, and it is considered the largest military exercise in the history of the region. The strategic land area chose to perform the exercise is Hafr Al-Batin, located in northern Saudi Arabia, which borders Iraq and is in close proximity to Syria.[38] Hamdan Al-Shehri, a political analyst, said, "The maneuver, which is a strong message for Iran, seeks to unify the military forces of Arab and Islamic countries."[39] Ahmad Assiri, a spokesman for the Arab coalition forces, said, "the aim of the exercise is to achieve the highest level of preparedness, exchange expertise, and promote coordination among the participating countries."[40]

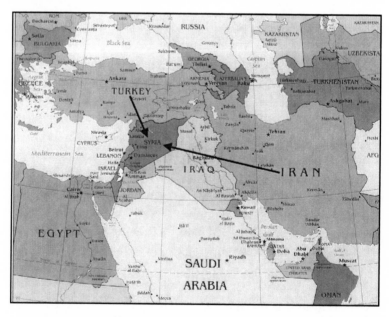

The Next Great Battle of the Middle East

It is important to understand that the battlefront of the Syrian civil war could very well dictate and set into motion the "next great war." This possibility would conclude with the rise of the Grecian Empire (Turkey) to Middle East dominance and supremacy and the dethroning of the Medo-Persian Empire (Iran). Looking at the map on page 71, we can see how Iran has marched across the Middle East and controlled much of Yemen, Iraq, Lebanon, and now its focus is on Syria. However, Turkey is rising to power with its allies (Saudi Arabia), and the stage is set for an epic Middle Eastern war of supremacy of biblical proportions.

SIGNS OF THE NEXT GREAT WAR BETWEEN IRAN AND TURKEY

On August 24, 2016, something very interesting occurred not only historically, but perhaps prophetically, as well. To be clear, I am not predicting or setting any dates whatsoever; however, August 24, 1516, is the historical date when the Ottoman Empire (Turkey) began their dominance and control over the Middle East at the Battle of Dabiq, in *Syria*.[41] The Ottomans defeated the Mamluk Sultanate and continued to rule over the Middle East for four hundred years.

On August 24, 2016, to celebrate the 500th anniversary of the Battle of Dabiq in Syria, Turkey (Ottoman Empire) has begun its largest intervention in Syria via a land invasion, which *could* be the spark that *eventually* lights the flame to the next great war in Daniel 8. Remember, Iran is a supporter of President Assad, and the Ayatollah has major influence in Syria, including the deployment of weapons, troops, and support during the ongoing civil war. Turkey, however, does not support Assad and Syria; thus the escalation of the invasion. As Turkish tanks entered Syria on August 24, 2016, Erdogan boldly proclaimed:

"Syria is responsible for the terrorism since it refuses to accept our solutions . . . When we speak of Syria or the Balkans or the Caucasus, these were part of our [Ottoman] geography from 100 years ago. I believe we will overcome all the obstacles in front of us, which will be the will of Allah . . . . Turkey has a massive power and will use it ... *We are more confident today about our future because since the morning of July the 15th (Turkey coup), we are more powerful, we are now in a place that looks more hopeful . . . Our commitment in achieving the 2023 target.* Turkey will cut off the front foot with the diplomatic games. We will continue to remove, those who played their games." Erdogan continued to add, "what I promised in Syria, Iraq, the Balkans and the Caucasus is now within reach."[42]

In 1516, the battle was called the Battle of Dabiq, and in 2016, it is being called "Operation Euphrates Shield." The Euphrates Shield is correlated with the memory of the Ottoman invasion of Syria at Dabiq. August 24, 2016, the 500th anniversary, *could* have set the stage and prepared the way for the next great war of Daniel 8.

HOW DOES THE BATTLE OF DABIQ RELATE TURKEY TO ISIS?

Although world leaders and the mainstream media speak of an ISIS caliphate in the Middle East, it is not biblical, as ISIS will eventually fall under Turkey's caliphate and dominant reign. In fact, in July of 2015, as the United States special forces raided a compound housing Abu Sayyaf, the ISIS chief financial officer, they produced evidence that Turkish officials directly dealt with ranking ISIS members. Make no mistake, Turkey is and will be the leader of the Islamic caliphate, just as the Biblical prophets foretold.

So what is Dabiq to ISIS and Turkey? Why is the invasion called "Operation Euphrates Shield"?

A CERTAIN ARABIC SOURCE STATES:

"The use of Dabiq by Isis is symbolic of the major historical event at Dabiq, it is the name of the battle the Ottomans (Turkey) won which paved the way for their occupation of Iraq and the Levant for more than four centuries, as well as being the springboard for the Islamic armies to fight the Rum (Romans/Europeans) in their quest for world domination."[43]

Furthermore, ISIS' television station is called "Dabiq," and the terror group calls its magazine *Dabiq*, dedicating it to the Ottoman (Turkey) victory at Dabiq, Syria. Even the ISIS flag is an Ottoman (Turkish) insignia, which is the insignia of Islam's prophet Muhammad's ring, which comes from the Turkish Topkapi museum; Everything about ISIS correlates to Dabiq, which is in honor of the Ottoman Empire (Turkey).

Turkey's invasion of Syria on August 24, 2016, *could* be the *very beginning* of Daniel 8, especially since Erdogan has declared that his goal for the "revived Ottoman Empire" is by the year 2023. Again, I am not setting dates in any way, but it would be wise to watch how the events unfold with Turkey in Syria. The battlefront of the Syrian civil war could very well dictate and set into motion the supreme dominance of the Grecian Empire (Turkey) and the fall of the Medo-Persian Empire (Iran) by 2023.

Below is a summary of the alliances of the Medo-Persian Empire (Iran) and the Grecian Empire (Turkey).

Medo-Persian Empire (Iran) Alliances:

- Russia
- China
- Lebanon (Hezbollah)
- Hamas
- Syria (Assad)

Grecian Empire (Turkey) Alliances:

- Saudi Arabia (North Thunder)
- ISIS

CONCLUSION

To be clear, although the Antichrist will rise from Turkey (Seleucid), Erdogan is *not* the Antichrist. As much as he proclaims to be god, and his supporters, including Saudi Arabia, flatter him like he is god, he is actually just a foreshadow of the Antichrist to come. Erdogan entering the gates to the Kaaba is just another interesting step toward the actual rise of the Antichrist's kingdom (Turkey).

However, since we are currently living in the Medo-Persian Empire (Iran) on God's prophetic timeline, I personally believe that Erdogan is the "large notable horn," or the first king of the Grecian Empire that Gabriel prophesied about in Daniel 8 (Dan. 8:21–22). As we have discovered, once the Grecian Empire (Turkey) rises to power and strength, the notable horn will be broken (dies), and the Grecian Empire will split into four regions. Then, the Antichrist will rise to power from the Seleucid division of the empire. Below is a summary of the events in exact order of Daniel 2, 7 and 8.

GOD'S PROPHETIC TIMELINE:

1. 1948 Prophecy - Fulfilled
2. 1967 Prophecy - Fulfilled
3. Babylonian Empire - Fulfilled
4. Medo-Persian Empire - Currently (2016)
5. Grecian Empire > Large horn broken (leader dies) > four smaller regions > Ten kings > Antichrist will rise (Seleucid division)
6. Antichrist's Kingdom (ten kings) = seven-year tribulation
7. Messiah's Second Coming
8. Millennial Reign
9. The New Jerusalem

CHAPTER 7

THE ANTICHRIST'S KINGDOM

Once the Grecian Empire (Turkey) rises to power in the Middle East, and the large horn (first king) is broken (leader dies), the kingdom will be divided into four regions. Soon after, an infamous man called the Antichrist will rise to power from the Grecian Empire (Seleucid division) and rule over the ten kings. Please note, before the Antichrist rises to power, the ten kings will have already been placed into their prophetic positions at the end of the age.

> Daniel 7:23–24, "The fourth beast shall be a fourth kingdom on earth, which shall be different from all other kingdoms, and shall devour the whole earth, trample it and break it in pieces. *The ten horns are ten kings who shall arise from this kingdom. And another shall rise after them*; He shall be different from the first ones, and shall subdue three kings."

As we have discovered in previous chapters, the kingdom after the Grecian Empire is the Antichrist's kingdom (fourth kingdom). Just as Daniel prophesied, the ten kings (horns) will be in power when the Antichrist rises to his prophetic calling (Rev. 17:12), and he will subdue three of the kings. Throughout history, there has been much debate about who the ten kings are, and where on Earth they will be located. By exploring the prophecies of the Holy Bible, we will be able to clearly understand what region the ten kings of the Antichrist's kingdom will be located. Before we discover the ten king's region, let us review in summary the foundation of the Antichrist's kingdom in Daniel 2 and Daniel 7.

Daniel 2:40, "And the *fourth kingdom* shall be as strong as iron, inasmuch as iron breaks in pieces and shatters everything; and like iron that crushes, *that kingdom will break in pieces and crush all the others.*"

Daniel 7:17, "Those great beasts, which are four, are *four kings* which arise out of the earth."

DANIEL 2'S METAL COMPONENTS (KINGDOMS)

1. Babylonian Empire (Iraq)-Fulfilled
2. Medo-Persian Empire (Iran) > 2016
3. Grecian Empire (Turkey)
4. Antichrist's Kingdom (ten kings)

DANIEL 7'S BEASTS (KINGDOMS)

1. Babylonian Empire (Iraq)-Fulfilled
2. Medo-Persian Empire (Iran) > 2016
3. Grecian Empire (Turkey)
4. Antichrist's Kingdom (ten kings)

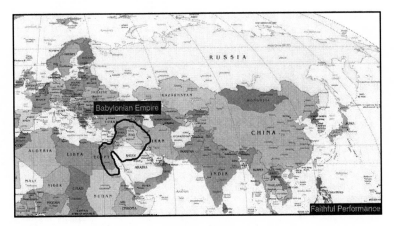

Babylonian Empire

Medo-Persian Empire

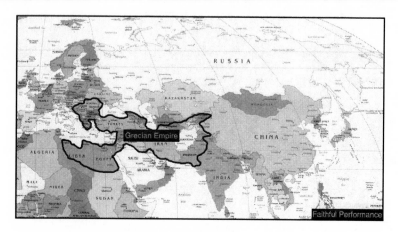

Grecian Empire

It is important to remember that Daniel prophesied that only *four kingdoms* will rise out of the Earth, and the Antichrist's kingdom will be the fourth. From the ancient maps, we can see that the first three kingdoms, the Babylonian, Medo-Persian, and Grecian Empires, primarily ruled over the same land area because they conquered one another. Although the conquering empire expanded the geographical region of the previous empire, these three kingdoms essentially ruled over the same regional area, which is located in the Middle East and North Africa. Now, let us explore Revelation 13 in order to gain great insight concerning the Antichrist's kingdom.

Revelation 13:1–2, "Then I stood on the sand of the sea. And I saw *a beast* rising up out of the sea, *having seven heads and ten horns, and on his horns ten crowns,* and on his heads a blasphemous name. Now the beast which I saw was like a *leopard,* his feet were like the feet of a *bear,* and his mouth like the mouth of a *lion.*"

John's vision in Revelation 13 describes *one beast* who looked like a *leopard* and had feet like a *bear* and a mouth like a *lion*. In Daniel 7, Daniel prophesied about *three separate beasts*, which are a *lion, a bear, and a leopard* (Dan. 7:2–8). What conclusions can we draw from Daniel 7 and Revelation 13?

In Daniel 7, the three separate beasts represent the three different kingdoms in the exact order that they will occur at the end of the age; Lion (Babylonian-Iraq), Bear (Medo-Persian-Iran), and Leopard (Grecian-Turkey). How does this correlate with John's vision in Revelation 13?

Revelation 13 describes *one beast* instead of three. John tells us that the one beast, which is the Antichrist's kingdom, will be a conglomerate of *all* of these kingdoms; Lion, Bear, and Leopard. In other words, the Antichrist's kingdom will be made up of the conglomerated land area of all of these kingdoms, because it is a lion, bear, and a leopard in *one beast* (kingdom). Remember, these three empires (Lion - Iraq, Bear - Iran, and Leopard - Turkey) primarily ruled over the same area, which is located in the Middle East and North Africa. The prophet Hosea confirms the Antichrist's conglomerated kingdom and land area (lion, bear, and leopard), as he prophesies to the children of Israel about the great tribulation period.

Hosea 13:7-8, "So I will be to them like a *lion*; Like a *leopard* by the road I will lurk; I will meet them like a *bear* deprived *of her cubs;* I will tear open their rib cage, and there I will devour them like a *lion*. The wild *beast* shall tear them.

Below is a summary of Daniel 2, Daniel 7, and Revelation 13.

DANIEL 2'S METAL COMPONENTS (KINGDOMS)

1.   Gold- Babylonian Empire (Iraq) - Fulfilled
2.   Silver- Medo-Persian Empire (Iran) > 2016
3.   Bronze- Grecian Empire (Turkey)
4.   Iron- Antichrist's Kingdom (ten kings)

DANIEL 7'S BEASTS

1.   Lion-Babylonian Empire (Iraq) - Fulfilled
2.   Bear-Medo-Persian Empire (Iran) > 2016
3.   Leopard-Grecian Empire (Turkey)
4.   Iron-Antichrist kingdom (ten kings)

REVELATION 13 "ONE BEAST"

Lion (Babylon), Bear (Persia), and Leopard (Grecian) = Antichrist's kingdom

Looking at the maps, if Revelation 13 is explaining that the Antichrist's kingdom (one beast) is a conglomerate of the Lion (Iraq), Bear (Iran), and Leopard (Turkey) kingdoms, then the ten kings of the Antichrist's kingdom will rise from the conglomerated land area of these three kingdoms! Daniel tells us who three of the ten kings are, because the Antichrist will conquer them (Daniel 7:24).

> Daniel 11:43, "He shall have power over the treasures of gold and silver, and over all the precious things of Egypt; also the Libyans and Ethiopians (Sudan) shall follow at his heels."

The Antichrist will conquer three of the ten kings during the seven-year tribulation period; Egypt, Libya, and Sudan. Ancient Ethiopia is modern-day Sudan (Cush). All three of these nations are located in the conglomerate land area of the ancient Babylonian, Medo-Persian, and Grecian Empires.

In summary, Daniel 7 describes three different beasts and Revelation 13 describes one beast, which tells us that the one beast, the Antichrist's kingdom, will be a conglomerate of all three of the kingdoms; Babylonian (Iraq), Persian (Iran), and Grecian (Turkey). When we review the ancient maps of these three empires and align them with the modern day map, it is clear that the ten kings will rise from the conglomerated land area of these three empires, which are today, Islamic Muslim nations.

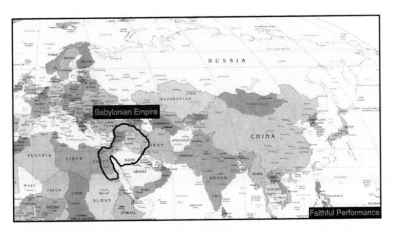

Babylonian Empire

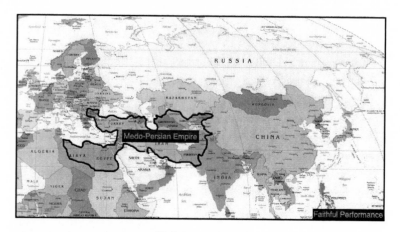

Medo-Persian Empire

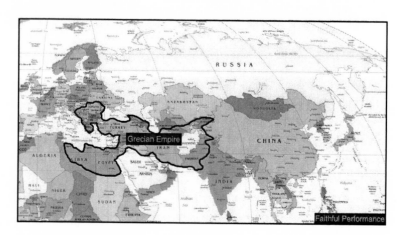

Grecian Empire

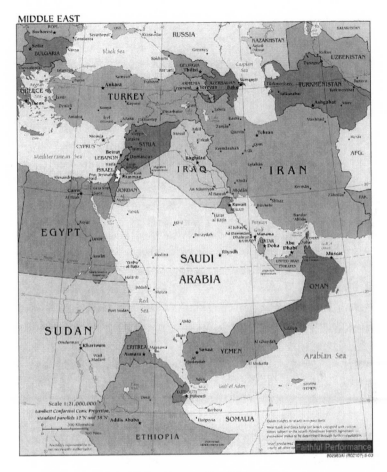

Middle East-Free map from biblesnet.com

REVELATION 17

Revelation 17 is another highly debated prophecy among Bible scholars and prophecy teachers. John's vision is of a woman and a beast who has seven heads and ten horns. Does Revelation 17 verify the prophecies of Daniel 2, 7, and 8 and Revelation 13? Does it also give us insight into the Antichrist's kingdom?

Revelation 17:3,7–8, "And I saw a woman sitting on a scarlet beast which was full of names of blasphemy, *having seven heads and ten horns.* But the angel said to me, "Why did you marvel? I will tell you the mystery of the woman and of the beast that carries her, which has the seven heads and the ten horns. *The beast that you saw was, and is not,* and will ascend out of the bottomless pit and go to perdition. And those who dwell on the earth will marvel, whose names are not written in the Book of Life from the foundation of the world, *when they see the beast that was, and is not, and yet is.*"

In Revelation 17, John describes a woman sitting on a beast who has seven heads and ten horns. He writes that it was *a beast,* meaning one beast, just as he described in Revelation 13. The ten horns of the beast represent the ten kings of the Antichrist's kingdom that we discovered in Daniel 2 (ten toes/kings), Daniel 7, and Revelation 13. John explains that the beast "was, and is not, and will ascend out of the bottomless pit and go to perdition." Please note that John lived during the Roman Empire. What wisdom and knowledge can we gain from John's riddle?

Here are the kingdoms in succession:

- Babylonian Empire
- Medo-Persian Empire
- Grecian Empire
- Roman Empire > John

John tells us the beast (Antichrist's kingdom- the conglomerate empires) "that was," which confirms that the three ancient kingdoms had fallen, and "is not," which means that they are no longer dominant, because the Roman Empire was in power during John's life. However, the beast (Antichrist's kingdom, the conglomerate empires) will rise again (yet is) out of the bottomless pit and go into perdition.

Revelation 17 is telling us that at the end of the age, the one beast, which is the conglomerated Babylonian, Medo-Persian, and Grecian Empires, will rise to power as the Antichrist's kingdom (10 kings). Nevertheless, at Messiah's Second Coming, the Antichrist's kingdom will go into perdition (lake of fire). Since Revelation 17 prophesies about the conglomerated Antichrist's kingdom, it confirms the Babylonian, Medo-Persian, and Grecian Empires of Daniel 2, Daniel 7, and Revelation 13!

Revelation 17:12–14, "*The ten horns which you saw are ten kings who have received no kingdom as yet, but they receive authority for one hour [7 years] as kings with the beast. These are of one mind, and they will give their power and authority to the beast.* These will make war with the Lamb, and the Lamb will overcome them, for He is Lord of lords and King of kings; and those who are with Him are called, chosen, and faithful." (emphasis mine)

As we discussed in Daniel 2, the ten toes (kings-Antichrist's kingdom) mixed with iron and clay (Sunni/Shiite) will come together as "one mind" to fight Messiah at His Second Coming. What about the seven heads of the beast in Revelation 17? How do they fit into the Antichrist's Kingdom?

First, it is important to understand that Daniel 7 prophesies about the beast with ten horns but it does not include the seven heads. However, John's vision of the beast in Revelation 17 includes ten horns and the seven heads. What does this imply?

The prophet Daniel lived in the Babylonian and Medo-Persian Empire, and he prophesied about the four kingdoms that will rise at the end of the age. John lived in the Roman Empire, and he prophesied about the world's seven major empires throughout history, beginning with the ancient Egyptian Empire and continuing through the Roman Empire, unto today.

Revelation 17:9–11, "Here is the mind which has wisdom: The *seven heads are seven mountains* on which the woman sits. There are also *seven kings. Five have fallen, one is, and the other has not yet come.* And when he comes, he must continue a short time. The beast that was, and is not, is himself also the eighth, and is of the seven, and is going to perdition."

In Revelation 17, John gives us a riddle to further confirm the region of the Antichrist's kingdom. He prophesies that the seven mountains (heads) have seven kings, which refers to seven kingdoms. As we discussed, mountains are symbolic for kingdoms (Isa. 2; Mic. 4; Dan. 2), since obviously, kings do not rule mountains, but they do rule kingdoms. John, who was living in the Roman Empire, explains that five kingdoms have already fallen before the Roman Empire. So, the sixth kingdom is the Roman Empire, and the seventh kingdom had yet to come. To solve the riddle, we need to find out who the seventh kingdom is, because it is also the eighth kingdom, and it is going to perdition. John gives us an essential clue about the seventh kingdom, as he writes, "when the empire comes, it will continue for a short time."

The question is, "What empire reigned after the Roman Empire and continued for a short time?"

The Seven Kingdoms (heads) of Revelation 17

1. Egyptian Empire
2. Assyrian Empire
3. Babylonian Empire
4. Medo-Persian Empire
5. Grecian Empire
6. Roman Empire > John
7. ?
8. Same as the seventh empire

The chart shows the natural succession of the kingdoms throughout world history in exact order. The renown historian Edward Gibbons gives us great insight into the fall of the Roman Empire, including the Eastern division.[1] In approximately AD 395, the Roman Empire was divided into two divisions; the eastern and western divisions. In 410, the western division, including the capital city of Rome, fell to invading Germanic tribes known as the Visigoths, or the Barbarians. Although the western division (European) fell, the eastern division still continued its reign. As the western division collapsed, the Roman Empire moved its capital a thousand miles east from Rome to Constantinople, which is now modern day Istanbul, Turkey, and it became known as the Byzantine Empire.

Although the western division fell, the eastern division (Byzantine) of the Roman Empire survived for another one thousand years, with the city of Constantinople as its capital. In 1453, the Eastern Roman Empire (Byzantine) completely fell to Mehmed II and the Ottoman Empire (Turkey). The Ottoman Empire continued to rule over the entire Middle East, including Jerusalem, for nearly five hundred years. The Ottoman Empire fell in 1923, fulfilling John's prophecy, "and when he comes, he must continue a short time." John confirms that the Ottoman Empire (Turkey) was "wounded" in 1923, but will rise again at the end of the age, which confirms Daniel 2, 7, and 8!

Revelation 13:3–4, "And I saw one of his heads (kingdoms) as if it had been mortally wounded, and his deadly wound was healed. And all the world marveled and followed the beast. So they worshiped the dragon who gave authority to the beast; and they worshiped the beast, saying, "Who is like the beast? Who is able to make war with him?"

John explains that one of the seven kingdoms (heads) was wounded, which was the Ottoman Empire (Turkey) in 1923, but the wound was healed. This gives us great knowledge that the Ottoman Empire (Turkey-Grecian Empire), who was wounded, will rise again at the end of the age. Revelation 17 not only correlates with Daniel 2, 7, 8, and Revelation 13, but it also aligns with what we discussed about Turkish President Erdogan and Turkey's (Ottoman Empire) rise to power. The Ottoman Empire is the seventh empire, and also the eighth, and it will go to perdition.

Revelation 17:11, "The beast that was, and is not, is himself also the eighth, and is of the seven, and is going to perdition."

Ottoman Empire

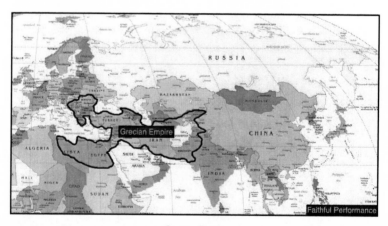

Grecian Empire

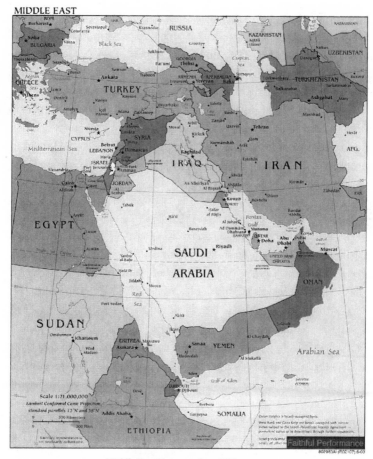

Middle East-Free map from biblesnet.com

It is imperative to understand that the Ottoman Empire (Turkey) and the Grecian Empire (Turkey) are interchangeable, because they essentially conquered and controlled the same land area. John's vision occurred at a later time than Daniel's in order to give us more knowledge and understanding from the dominance of the Roman Empire. However, it still confirms that the Antichrist's kingdom will be a conglomerate of the Babylonian, Medo-Persian, and Grecian

Empires. (Please note, the first two empires, the ancient Egyptian and Assyrian Empires, are also located in the conglomerated land area of the Antichrist's kingdom). In Revelation 17, the Ottoman Empire confirms the conglomerate land area of the three ancient empires of Daniel, which will form the Antichrist's kingdom.

Now that we understand that the ten kings of the Antichrist kingdom will rise in the Middle East and North Africa (Egypt, Libya, Sudan), let us explore what the Biblical prophets, Isaiah, Jeremiah, and Ezekiel wrote in order to confirm this, as well.

ISAIAH

In Isaiah chapters 13 through 23, Isaiah proclaims the Lord's judgment against the following nations: Babylon (Iraq), Assyria (Syria), Philistia (Gaza), Moab (Jordan), Ethiopia (Sudan), Egypt, Edom (Jordan/Saudi Arabia), Shebna, and Tyre (Lebanon). The context of Isaiah's oracles is clearly describing the Day of the Lord, because he repeatedly states "in that day, in that day." The phrase, "in that day" is an eschatological term for the Day of the Lord, the Second Coming of Messiah. Comparing all of the countries except for Saudi Arabia to the map, it is clear that Isaiah gives us confirmation about the land area of the ten kings of the Antichrist's kingdom that Messiah will send to perdition at His Second Coming.

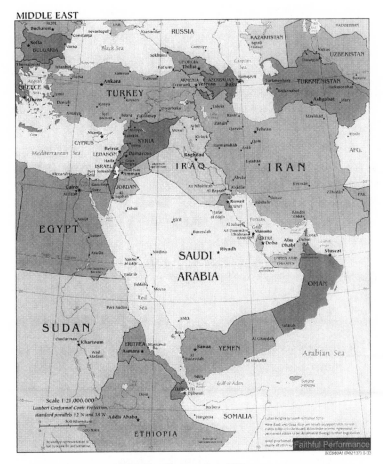

Middle East-Free map from biblesnet.com

JEREMIAH

In Jeremiah 25:15–37, Jeremiah proclaims the Lord's judgment against the following nations; Egypt, the kings of the land of Uz (Jordan/Saudi Arabia), the Philistines (Gaza), Edom (Jordan/Saudi Arabia), Moab (Jordan), Ammon (Jordan), Tyre (Lebanon), Sidon (Lebanon), Dedan (Saudi Arabia), Tema (Saudi Arabia), Elam (Iran),

Medes (Kurds-northern Iraq), and the king of the north (Turkey). The context of Jeremiah's prophecy points to the end of the age, because he speaks of the seven-year tribulation and Messiah's Second Coming, along with the judgments of the nations (Jer. 25:30–33). Jeremiah confirms *some* of the ten kings of the Antichrist's kingdom, excluding Saudi Arabia, which will be destroyed at Messiah's Second Coming, as well.

Also, in Jeremiah chapters 46 through 51, he proclaims the Lord's judgment against the following nations: Egypt, Babylon (Iraq), Philistia (Gaza), Moab (Jordan), Ammon (Jordan), Edom (Jordan/Saudi Arabia), Syria, Kedar (Saudi Arabia), Hazor (Arab desert), and Elam (Iran). The context of Jeremiah's prophecies are "for this is the day of the Lord, a day of vengeance, and in that day," which clearly are eschatological terms that refers to the end of the age, Messiah's Second Coming.

EZEKIEL

In Ezekiel chapters 25 through 31, Ezekiel proclaims the Lord's judgment against the following nations; Ammon (Jordan), Moab (Jordan), Edom (Jordan/Saudi Arabia), Philistia (Gaza), Tyre (Lebanon), Sidon (Lebanon), Egypt, Sudan, Libya and Lydia (Turkey). In these prophetic chapters, Ezekiel uses the terms "Day of Vengeance and the Day of the Lord," which again are eschatological terms for the end of the age, Messiah's Second Coming. Also, in Ezekiel 32:18–32, Ezekiel tells us the specific nations that are consigned to hell (pit): Egypt, Syria, Iran, Turkey, Jordan, Saudi Arabia, and Lebanon. Certainly, some of these nations, excluding Saudi Arabia, will be included in the Antichrist's kingdom.

Isaiah, Jeremiah, and Ezekiel give us great insight into some of the countries that will form the Antichrist's kingdom, as they are located in the conglomerated land area of the ancient Babylonian, Medo-Persian, and Grecian kingdoms. Without question, these nations, except for Saudi Arabia, perfectly align with the conglomerate land area of the ancient kingdoms in Daniel 2, 7 and 8, and Revelation 13 and 17.

Isaiah 46:9–10, "Remember the former things of old, for I am God, and there is no other; I am God, and there is none like Me, *declaring the end from the beginning, and from ancient times things that are not yet done*, saying, 'My counsel shall stand, and I will do all My pleasure.'"

Ecclesiastes 1:9–10, "That which has been is what will be, that which is done is what will be done, and there is nothing new under the sun. Is there anything of which it may be said, "See, this is new?"

If God is declaring the end from the beginning, and He has given us the prophetic foreshadows of Daniel 2, 7 and 8, Revelation 13 and 17, and also great wisdom through the other Biblical prophets, then the conglomerated land area of the ancient Babylonian, Medo-Persian, and Grecian Empires (Ottoman) will form the ten kings of the Antichrist kingdom.

CONCLUSION

It is imperative to understand that the Promised Land of Israel, including the holy city of Jerusalem, is the primary region in the Holy Bible. The ultimate story throughout the Holy Bible is written about God's chosen heritage, land, and people, and their eternal enemies, whom we know today as Islamic Muslims. The final battle is for the possession of Jerusalem, because Satan wants to conquer the Promised Land, including Zion, because this is where God has cemented His name with His everlasting covenants and it is where He dwells!

Joel 3:17, 21, "So you shall know that I am the Lord your God, dwelling in Zion My holy mountain. Then Jerusalem shall be holy, and no aliens shall ever pass through her again. *For the Lord dwells in Zion.*"

God has given us prophetic foreshadows and prophecies to help us understand where the Antichrist's kingdom will be located. According to the Scriptures, the Antichrist's kingdom points directly to the Islamic Muslim countries that surrounds the Promised Land today. From the beginning until Messiah's Second Coming, the ultimate battle will be between Messiah and Satan, through Isaac and Ishmael, Jacob (Israel) and Esau (Edom), and their descendants, culminating with Judeo (Jews)-Christianity and Islam. Will there be other nations that support the Antichrist's kingdom? Absolutely. In fact, the whole world will be involved in the great Battle of Armageddon. However, according to God's prophets, the ten kings will be a conglomerate kingdom consisting of the land area of the ancient Babylonian, Medo-Persian, and Grecian Empires

With the wisdom, knowledge, and understanding of the conglomerate land area of the Antichrist's kingdom, the question remains, "who are the ten kings?" Just as Daniel prophesied, three of the ten kings will be Egypt, Libya, and Sudan (Dan. 11:43). One thing to keep in mind about the ten kings of the Antichrist's kingdom is that the Grecian Empire will split into four smaller kingdoms, so those kings will be four of the ten kings (Daniel 8:8).

In other words, if four horns come up after the large horn is broken, and horns represent kings (Dan. 8:22), then these four kings will be four of the ten kings of the Antichrist's kingdom. So, with the knowledge of seven of the ten kings, Egypt, Libya, Sudan, and four from the divided Grecian Empire, we can only watch the conglomerated land area to see who the other three kings will be. The important concept to remember is that the ten kings of the Antichrist's kingdom will rise from the conglomerated land area of the ancient Babylonian, Medo-Persian, and Grecian Empires. Here is a list of countries in the conglomerated area:

Egypt (one king), Libya (one king), Sudan (one king), Turkey's four regions (four kings), Iraq, Iran, Lebanon, Jordan, Syria, Afghanistan, and Pakistan. These are all Islamic Muslim countries. Please note, not all of the Arabs in these locations are Muslims, as hundreds of thousands are saved in Messiah! Hallelujah!

What about Saudi Arabia? What is its' role and destiny on God's prophetic timeline?

CHAPTER 8

MYSTERY, BABYLON THE GREAT, THE MOTHER OF HARLOTS

"Mystery, Babylon the Great, the Mother of Harlots" is a mystery to the world! Some Bible scholars and prophecy teachers believe that Mystery Babylon is the Catholic Church (Vatican), the city of New York, the United States of America, or some other popular place. However, when we search the Biblical prophet's writings, those assumptions are based upon unbiblical theories and prejudices.

It is important to understand that the Holy Bible was inspired and written in an Israel-centric theme, not a European or American theme. Just as we discovered in the previous chapter, this is ultimately a war between God and Satan, Jesus and the Antichrist, Isaac and Ishmael, Jacob (Israel) and Esau (Edom), and their descendants. We must always remember to look at the Scriptures with a "Middle Eastern lens" first before we apply them to our Western mindset. With this in mind, let us explore the biblical prophets to understand who is Mystery Babylon, where the "Mother of Harlots" is located, and how this wicked pagan country will be destroyed!

> Revelation 17:3–5, "And I saw a woman sitting on a scarlet beast which was full of names of blasphemy, having seven heads and ten horns. The woman was arrayed in purple and scarlet, and adorned with gold and precious stones and

pearls, having in her hand a golden cup full of abominations and the filthiness of her fornication. And on her forehead a name was written: MYSTERY, BABYLON THE GREAT, THE MOTHER OF HARLOTS AND OF THE ABOMINATIONS OF THE EARTH."

In John's vision, he saw a woman who spoke blasphemy seated on a scarlet beast with seven heads and ten horns. In the previous chapter, we discovered the ten horns and seven heads of the scarlet beast, which is the Antichrist's kingdom (conglomerated Babylonian, Medo-Persian, and Grecian Empires). In this chapter, we will focus on the woman who is sitting on the beast. Although John's vision and writings of Mystery Babylon is the most well known to believers, Mystery Babylon is first prophesied in the book of Isaiah.

Isaiah 21:1–2,5–7, "The burden against the Wilderness of the Sea. As whirlwinds in the South pass through, so it comes from the desert, from a terrible land. A distressing vision is declared to me; The treacherous dealer deals treacherously, and the plunderer plunders. Go up, O Elam! Besiege, O Media! Prepare the table, set a watchman in the tower, eat and drink. Arise, you princes, Anoint the shield! For thus has the Lord said to me: "Go, set a watchman, let him declare what he sees." And he saw a chariot with a pair of horsemen, a chariot of donkeys, and a chariot of camels, and he listened earnestly with great care."

Isaiah's oracle of Mystery Babylon begins as he declares that the judgment is against the "Wilderness of the Sea." In *Strong's* dictionary #6160, the Hebrew word for wilderness is *desert*, so the judgment is against the "Desert of the Sea." As the prophecy continues, Isaiah reveals that Elam (Iran) and the Medes (Kurds) will destroy the harlot, Mystery Babylon. It is the widely held belief that Isaiah's prophecy was fulfilled when the ancient Medo-Persian Empire (Kurds/Iran) destroyed ancient Babylon in 539 BC (Dan. 5). However, is Isaiah 21 ultimately an end of the age prophecy?

At the beginning of the prophecy, Isaiah states that the judgment is against the "Desert of the Sea." When we review the maps, Isaiah 21 cannot be prophesying of ancient Babylon, as it is not surrounded by any sea, only by the Tigris and Euphrates rivers.

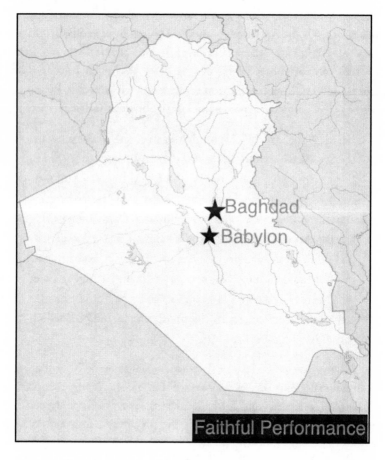

Iraq

Babylonian Empire

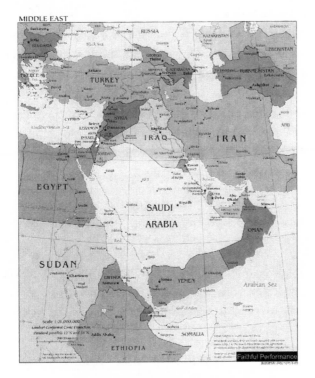

Middle East-Free map from biblesnet.com

Isaiah 21:9–17, "Then he answered and said, "Babylon is fallen, is fallen! And all the carved images of her gods He has broken to the ground." Oh, my threshing and the grain of my floor. That which I have heard from the Lord of hosts, the God of Israel, I have declared to you. Proclamation against Edom the burden against Dumah, He calls to me out of Seir, "Watchman, what of the night? Watchman, what of the night?" The watchman said, "The morning comes, and also the night. If you will inquire, inquire; Return! Come back!" Proclamation against Arabia, the burden against Arabia. In the forest in Arabia you will lodge, O you traveling companies of Dedanites. O inhabitants of the land of Teman. Bring water to him who is thirsty; With their bread they met him who fled for they fled from the swords, from the drawn sword, From the bent bow, and from the distress of war. For thus the Lord has said to me: "Within a year, according to the year of a hired man, all the glory of Kedar will fail; and the remainder of the number of archers, the mighty men of the people of Kedar, will be diminished; for the Lord God of Israel has spoken it." Isaiah continues his prophecy by stating, "Babylon is fallen, is fallen!"

Isaiah 21 continues with a direct parallel to John's proclamation, "Babylon is fallen, is fallen," linking these two end of the age prophecies together.

Revelation 14:8, "And another angel followed, saying, "Babylon is fallen, is fallen, that great city, because she has made all nations drink of the wine of the wrath of her fornication."

Revelation 18:2, "And he cried mightily with a loud voice, saying, "Babylon the great is fallen, is fallen."

Isaiah also reveals the location of Mystery Babylon by specifically naming the locations whom the judgment is proclaimed against: Edom, Dumah, Seir, Arabia, Teman, and Kedar. These literal referenced locations are not in Rome, America, or anywhere else, but are all located in Saudi Arabia! Saudi Arabia is Mystery Babylon the Great, the Mother of Harlots! Isaiah solves the mystery for us by including the name "Arabia" in his oracle and also states that the Dedanites will lodge in the "desert of Arabia."

The location of Edom (Esau) is another debated topic, as some believe it is only located in Jordan. However, the prophet Ezekiel describes in detail its proximity, and confirms Edom is mostly located in Saudi Arabia.

Ezekiel 25:13, "Therefore thus says the Lord God: 'I will stretch My hand against Edom, cut off man and beast from it, and make it desolate from Teman; Dedan shall fall by the sword.'"

Location of Edom

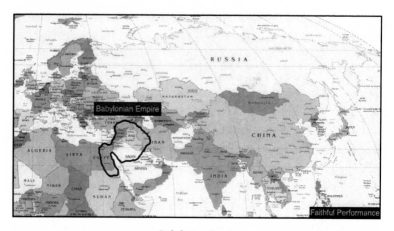

Babylonian Empire

Middle East-Free map from biblesnet.com

Ezekiel states that Edom is the area from Yemen (Teman) to Dedan (Edom included all of the west coast of the Arabian Peninsula). Dumah, Seir, Kedar, and Dedan are all located in Saudi Arabia and not ancient Babylon. Also, Saudi Arabia was included in the ancient Babylonian Empire, as Edom (Saudi Arabia) is referred to as the "daughter of Babylon."

> Psalm 137:7–8, "Remember, O Lord, against the sons of Edom, the day of Jerusalem, Who said, "Raze it, raze it, to its very foundation!" O daughter of Babylon, who are to be destroyed."

The psalmist prophesies that at the day of Jerusalem (Messiah's Second Coming), "O daughter of Babylon will be destroyed," referring to Saudi Arabia. The day of Jerusalem is an eschatological term for Messiah's Second Coming, when He will fight, conquer, and rule over the holy city for His millennial reign. Jeremiah prophesies about Messiah's judgment on Edom and Bozrah (Saudi Arabia), and confirms the location of the "Desert by the Sea."

> Jeremiah 49:20–22, "Therefore hear the counsel of the Lord that He has taken against Edom, and His purposes that He has proposed against the inhabitants of Teman: Surely the least of the flock shall draw them out; Surely He shall make their dwelling places desolate with them. The earth shakes at the noise of their fall; At the cry its noise is heard at the *Red Sea*. Behold, He shall come up and fly like the eagle, and spread His wings over Bozrah; The heart of the mighty men of Edom in that day shall be like the heart of a woman in birth pangs."

Jeremiah prophesies that Messiah will fly like an eagle and spread His wings of destruction over Edom, Teman, and Bozrah, which are all located in Saudi Arabia. Jeremiah's oracle places this event at Messiah's Second Coming, His day of vengeance. He also states, "the cry from its destruction will be heard at the red sea," which is another confirmation that Saudi Arabia is Mystery Babylon, as it is located next to the biblically famous sea. Isaiah also declares Messiah's judgment on Saudi Arabia, the great harlot.

> Isaiah 63:1–4, "Who is this who comes from Edom, with dyed garments from Bozrah, this One who is glorious in His apparel, traveling in the greatness of His strength? "I who speak in righteousness, mighty to save. Why is Your apparel red, and Your garments like one who treads in the winepress? "I have trodden the winepress alone, and from the peoples' no one was with Me. For I have trodden them in My anger, and trampled them in My fury; Their blood is sprinkled upon My garments, and I have stained all My robes. For the day of vengeance is in My heart, and the year of My redeemed has come."

Isaiah's prophecy places Messiah on Earth during His Second Coming in Edom and Bozrah, which are located in Saudi Arabia. Needless to say, the Lion of Judah is coming for His day of vengeance, as He will trample the winepress in His fury, and the blood will be sprinkled upon His garments, staining His robe. In Revelation 17, John also confirms the harlot's location, as well.

> Revelation 17:1–3, "Then one of the seven angels who had the seven bowls came and talked with me, saying to me, "Come, I will show you the judgment of the great harlot who sits on many waters, with whom the kings of the earth committed fornication, and the inhabitants of the earth were made drunk with the wine of her fornication. So he carried me away in the Spirit into the wilderness."

The angel carried John to the desert to show him the judgment of the great harlot who sits on many waters. Remember, ancient Babylon was located on two rivers, the Euphrates and the Tigris. Saudi Arabia (Mystery Babylon) is surrounded by many waters that includes; The Arabian Sea, Persian Gulf, Gulf of Oman, Gulf of Aden, and the Red Sea, confirming Jeremiah's prophecy of the Red Sea, as well (Jer. 49:20–22).

Jeremiah 51:13, "O you who dwell by many waters, abundant in treasures, your end has come."

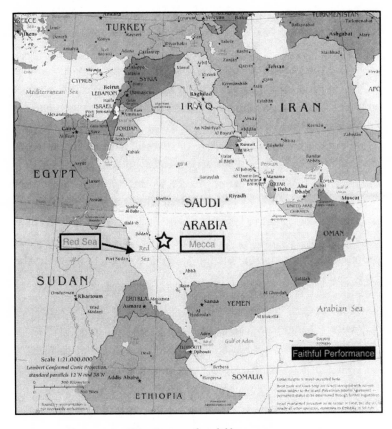

Mecca-Free map from biblesnet.com

Please note that Mecca, Saudi Arabia, the holiest city in Islam and the worst blasphemy to Judeo-Christianity, is located very close to the Red Sea. Furthermore, the Islamic nations commonly refer to Saudi Arabia as the "Arab Island," as there are many waters that surround it.[1]

In Revelation 17:2, John continues to tell us that the harlot will make the nations drunk off their "wine." I believe that we can agree that "good wine" does not come from Saudi Arabia or from any other country that would be good enough to make the inhabitants of the whole world drunk! John used wine as symbolism in this Scripture, because the product he was speaking of was not produced during his time. So, what product does make the inhabitants of the whole world "drunk?"

Yes, you guessed it: **oil!** The world is addicted to oil and it is the number-one product that causes the world to commit spiritual fornication. All of the world's leaders (kings) are fighting, scheming, maneuvering, and "committing fornication" with Saudi Arabia for its main source, oil. As the harlot sells more oil, she can advance her blasphemous, radical agenda of Islam, which is the main "spiritual fornication" of the world. Spiritual fornication also refers to the nations' betrayal of God's covenanted people (Israel) for oil as they pledge their support to Saudi Arabia, indulging and advancing the harlot's agenda. The prophet Joel prophesied about the blasphemous alliance of the nations to the great harlot, as well.

Joel 3:1–3, "For behold, in those days and at that time, when I bring back the captives of Judah and Jerusalem, I will also gather all nations, and bring them down to the Valley of Jehoshaphat; And I will enter into judgment with them there on account of My people, My heritage Israel, whom they have scattered among the nations; They have also divided up My land. They have cast lots for My people, have given a boy as payment for a harlot, and sold a girl for **wine**, that they may drink." (emphasis mine)

Did you catch the last sentence? Clearly, the Lord will judge **all** nations who have scattered His people across the world, divided His land, and have "sold out" His children for oil (wine). Certainly, it is safe to say that Isaiah and Joel did not know what oil is, as it was not discovered until three thousand years after they both lived on Earth. Also, the apostle John, who lived two thousand years before the discovery of oil, confirms the world's addiction to it.

Revelation 18:3, "For all the nations have drunk of the wine of the wrath of her fornication, the kings of the earth have committed fornication with her, and the merchants of the earth have become rich, through the abundance of her luxury."

What country do all other nations in the world mostly depend on for oil (wine)? The resounding answer is Saudi Arabia, the mother of harlots! Saudi Arabia has one-fourth of the world's oil reserves, and as of 2013, they were the largest exporter of oil in the world, producing 10.3 million barrels a day![2] Make no mistake, there is not another product in the world that is as vital to the nations as oil (wine), and Saudi Arabia is the number-one exporter, as the kings of the earth are made drunk, committing spiritual fornication. It is estimated that Saudi Arabia makes approximately a **billion** dollars a day. That is right, a billion! Saudi Arabia lives in the abundance of luxury, and the merchants of the Earth have become rich, as well. The world has become so addicted to oil, riches, and luxurious living, that Saudi Arabia has and will have major influence in the political and spiritual realms of all nations (spiritual fornication), just as John prophesied.

In fact, we are already seeing this today, as the mainstream media outlets do not report the suppressed culture of Saudi Arabia, including the heinous and outrageous beheadings,[3] suppression of women's rights,[4] human rights abuses[5], and the discrimination of religious liberties[6], which includes attacks on Jews and Christians. Furthermore, Saudi Arabia does not allow churches to be built, and if a person is caught sharing the gospel of Messiah, they may be sentenced to prison or beheaded[7]. All of these horrific acts are either not reported or misrepresented, as the world leaders "drink" the oil of Saudi Arabia's fornication. Also, we have to remember that Mecca, the number-one site in Islam, is located in Saudi Arabia, the largest "spiritual fornication" of the world. Isaiah prophesied about God's judgment on the nations, including the harlot, Saudi Arabia (Edom).

> Isaiah 34:5, 8–10, "For My sword shall be bathed in heaven; Indeed, it shall come down on Edom, and on the people of My curse, for judgment. For it is the day of the Lord's vengeance, the year of recompense for the cause of Zion. Its streams shall be turned into pitch, and its dust into brimstone; Its land shall become burning pitch. It shall not be quenched night or day; Its smoke shall ascend forever. From generation to generation it shall lie waste; No one shall pass through it forever and ever."

Isaiah's prophecy confirms the Lord's judgment on Saudi Arabia (Edom) at the day of the Lord's vengeance, which is an eschatological term referring to Messiah's Second Coming. He also states that "its streams shall be turned to pitch, and dust into brimstone, becoming an everlasting burning pitch." This certainly substantiates the fact that ancient Babylon is not Mystery Babylon, as modern-day Iraq does not have burning streams of pitch since ancient Babylon collapsed (539 BC). Also, Iraq is inhabited and people "pass through" the country. Ezekiel supports Isaiah's prophecy of the devastation to Saudi Arabia (Mystery Babylon).

Ezekiel 20:47–49, "Thus says the Lord God: "Behold, I will kindle a fire in you, and it shall devour every green tree and every dry tree in you; the blazing flame shall not be quenched, and all faces from the south to the north shall be scorched by it. All flesh shall see that I, the Lord, have kindled it; it shall not be quenched.""

In Isaiah's and Ezekiel's prophecies of judgment against Mystery Babylon, the prophets give great insight into Saudi Arabia's destruction. Oil is the only product in the world that could fulfill these prophecies. It is the only product that could burn land forever and ever, turning it into a burning pitch that will never be quenched from generation to generation. We can imagine this apocalyptic scene as we recall Saddam Hussein setting the oil fields on fire in Kuwait during the first Gulf War (1990–1991). The oil fields streamed and burned with fire and black smoke (burning pitch), turning the skies dark as night. Similarly, albeit on a much larger apocalyptic scale, so shall it be on Saudi Arabia at the day of the Lord's vengeance, His Second Coming!

Revelation 18:8–10, "Therefore her plagues will come in **one day**—death and mourning and famine. And she will be utterly burned with fire, for strong is the Lord God who judge her. The kings of the earth who committed fornication and lived luxuriously with her will weep and lament for her, when they see the smoke of her burning, standing at a distance for fear of her torment, saying, 'Alas, alas, that great city Babylon, that mighty city! For in **one hour** your judgment has come." (emphasis mine)

John prophesies that the judgment of Mystery Babylon the harlot will occur in one day, which will be Messiah's Second Coming. This event has not happened yet because at the time of John's writing, mankind could not destroy a city in one day. Even today, only a nuclear weapon could achieve this type of destruction. Nonetheless, Mystery Babylon, the Great the Mother of Harlots (Saudi Arabia), will be destroyed by fire on the Day of the Lord, Messiah's Second Coming (Rev. 14:14–16).

> Jeremiah 50:39–40, "It shall be inhabited no more forever, nor shall it be dwelt in from generation to generation. As God overthrew Sodom and Gomorrah and their neighbors," says the Lord, "So no one shall reside there, nor son of man dwell in it."

Sodom and Gomorrah are the only cities that have come under this type of judgment from the Lord (Gen. 18-19). However, Sodom and Gomorrah's judgment by fire did not ascend forever like the prophecies of Saudi Arabia state it will.

> Jeremiah 52:6–7, "For this is the time of the Lord's vengeance; He shall recompense her. Babylon was a golden cup in the Lord's hand, that made all the earth drunk. The nations drank her wine; Therefore, the nations are deranged. Babylon has suddenly fallen and been destroyed."

The day of the Lord's vengeance is an eschatological term for Messiah's Second Coming and it is how we can confirm that Jeremiah's prophecy is speaking of Saudi Arabia, not ancient Babylon. Also, this prophecy supports the other prophecies mentioned in this chapter, as Saudi Arabia has made all of the Earth drunk off the wine (oil) of its fornication. The prophets John, Isaiah and Jeremiah, explain that Saudi Arabia will become desolate, as nothing will dwell there but demons, evil spirits, wild beasts, jackals, and unclean birds.

> Revelation 18:2, "And he cried mightily with a loud voice, saying, "Babylon the great is fallen, is fallen, and has become

a dwelling place of demons, a prison for every foul spirit, and a cage for every unclean and hated bird!"

Isaiah 34:14, "The wild beasts of the desert shall also meet with the jackals, and the wild goat shall bleat to its companion; also the night creature shall rest there, and find for herself a place of rest."

Isaiah 13:19–22, "And Babylon, the glory of kingdoms, the beauty of the Chaldeans' pride, will be as when God overthrew Sodom and Gomorrah. It will never be inhabited, nor will it be settled from generation to generation; Nor will the Arabian pitch tents there, nor will the shepherds make their sheepfolds there. But wild beasts of the desert will lie there, and their houses will be full of owls; Ostriches will dwell there, and wild goats will caper there. The hyenas will howl in their citadels, and jackals in their pleasant palaces. Her time is near to come, and her days will not be prolonged."

Jeremiah 51:37, "Behold, I will plead your case and take vengeance for you. I will dry up her sea and make her springs dry. Babylon shall become a heap, a dwelling place for jackals, an astonishment and a hissing, without an inhabitant."

As we have discovered, the Lord will destroy the inhabitants of Saudi Arabia by the sword, as His garments are sprinkled with blood and His robe is stained from the winepress (Isa. 63:1–6). He will also destroy the land of Saudi Arabia by fire. Please note, at Messiah's Second Coming, there will be two sickles of judgment, one of the sword and the other of fire, as we will discuss in the next chapter (Revelation 14). It is important to understand that Isaiah, Jeremiah,

Ezekiel, Joel, and all of the prophets did not have any concept of nuclear weapons, so the only way they could describe this event was by fire. In Joel's prophetic book, he describes the wonders in the heavens and in the Earth that our generation can definitely relate to that will occur at Messiah's Second Coming.

Joel 2:30, "And I will show you wonders in the heavens and in the earth: Blood and fire and pillars of smoke.

Is Joel referring to the "pillars of smoke" of a nuclear bomb in the images below?

Pillars of Smoke

It is imperative to understand that Mystery Babylon the harlot (woman) is not the same as the beast, as they are two different entities. The harlot is Saudi Arabia and the beast is the Antichrist's kingdom that will consist of the ten kings.

> Revelation 17:3, "And I saw a woman sitting on a scarlet beast which was full of names of blasphemy, having seven heads and ten horns."

> Revelation 17:4–6, "The woman was arrayed in purple and scarlet, and adorned with gold and precious stones and pearls, having in her hand a golden cup full of abominations and the filthiness of her fornication. And on her forehead a name was written: MYSTERY, BABYLON THE GREAT, THE MOTHER OF HARLOTS AND OF THE ABOMINATIONS OF THE EARTH. I saw the woman, drunk with the blood of the saints and with the blood of the martyrs of Jesus. And when I saw her, I marveled with great amazement."

In John's vision of the woman (Saudi Arabia), he states that "she was drunk with the blood of the saints and with the martyrs of Jesus." Saudi Arabia is one of the worst countries, if not the worst, that persecutes Jews and Christians. They do not allow Jews and Christians to build churches or synagogues and the country is very segregated. Saudi Arabia directly supports terrorist's organizations, including ISIS, and is a radical, fundamentalist Islamic state. We never hear about the direct relationship with the terrorist's organizations, Christian martyrs, or the assault on Jews, because the mainstream media are controlled by the globalists (kings), who are drunk off of the wine (oil) of the harlots' spiritual fornication. Also Mecca (false religious harlot), which is the holiest site in Islam, is located in Saudi Arabia, the blasphemy of blasphemies to the Judeo-Christian faith (1 John 2:22–23).

If the ten kings of the Antichrist's kingdom are referred to as the beast, and the harlot is Saudi Arabia, what can we make of the woman sitting on the beast? What does this imply about the beast and the harlot's relationship at the end of the age?

> Revelation 17:16–17, "And the ten horns which you saw on the beast, these will **hate** the harlot, make her desolate and naked, eat her flesh and burn her with **fire**. For God has put it into their hearts to fulfill His purpose, to be of one mind, and to give their kingdom to the beast, until the words of God are fulfilled."

John confirms that the Antichrist's kingdom (ten kings) will *hate* the harlot and they will make her desolate, naked, and destroy her with fire. God will influence the ten kings of the Antichrist's kingdom and place in their heart to become of "one mind" to destroy the harlot, Saudi Arabia.

> Jeremiah 50:41–42, 46, "Behold, a people shall come from the north, and a great nation and many kings shall be raised up from the ends of the earth. They shall hold the bow and the lance; They are cruel and shall not show mercy. Their voice shall roar like the sea; Against you, O daughter of Babylon. At the noise of the taking of Babylon the earth trembles, and the cry is heard among the nations." (Also see Jer. 49:21)

As we have discovered in the previous chapter, the Antichrist's kingdom will be formed from the conglomerated Babylonian, Medo-Persian, and Grecian Empires, which are all predominantly north of Saudi Arabia. The Antichrist's kingdom (ten kings) will join together (one mind) and destroy Saudi Arabia, the harlot. After Messiah comes for His Second Coming with the sickle of the sword (Isa. 63:1–6, Rev. 19:13), what specific nations will He influence to destroy Saudi Arabia with the sickle of fire?

> Isaiah 21:1–2, "The burden against the Wilderness of the Sea. As whirlwinds in the South pass through, so it comes

from the desert, from a terrible land. A distressing vision is declared to me; The treacherous dealer deals treacherously, and the plunderer plunders. *Go up, O Elam! Besiege, O Media!* All its sighing I have made to cease."

Isaiah 13:17–20, "Behold, I will stir up the Medes against them, who will not regard silver; and as for gold, they will not delight in it. Also their bows will dash the young men to pieces, and they will have no pity on the fruit of the womb; Their eye will not spare children. And Babylon, the glory of kingdoms, the beauty of the Chaldeans' pride, will be as when God overthrew Sodom and Gomorrah. It will never be inhabited, nor will it be settled from generation to generation; nor will the Arabian pitch tents there, nor will the shepherds make their sheepfolds there."

The nations that will destroy Saudi Arabia by fire will be Iran (Elam) and the Kurds (Medes), who will be included in the Antichrist's kingdom. Please note, as of 2016, Iran's (Elam) main goal is to produce or buy nuclear weapons to fulfill their future prophetic mission. Saudi Arabia will have the same fate as Sodom and Gomorrah, as it will never be inhabited again and the Arabians will never "pitch their tents" in these areas again. At Messiah's Second Coming, once Saudi Arabia (Mystery Babylon) is destroyed, the heavens and the earth will worship, praise, and sing joyfully over the destruction of the harlot!

Revelation 19:1-5, "And after these things I heard a great voice of much people in heaven, saying, Alleluia; Salvation, and glory, and honor, and power, unto the Lord our God: For true and righteous are his judgments: for he hath judged the great whore, which did corrupt the earth with her fornication, and hath avenged the blood of his servants at her hand. And again they said, Alleluia. And her smoke rose up for ever and ever. And the four and twenty elders and the four beasts fell down and worshipped God that sat on the throne, saying, Amen; Alleluia. And a voice came out of the throne, saying, Praise our God, all ye his servants, and ye that fear him, both small and great."

CHAPTER 9

THE SECOND COMING

At the end of the age, once the ten kings of the Antichrist's kingdom are established, the Antichrist will rise to power and rule over them for the last seven years (Dan. 7:24, 9:27), which is the seven-year tribulation period. Simultaneously, the Antichrist will confirm a seven-year peace treaty with Israel and others, but he will break the covenant in the middle of its term (Dan. 7:25, 9:27, Dan. 12:7). This time period is commonly referred to as the great tribulation (Matthew 24:21–22). Nevertheless, at the end of the great tribulation (Rev. chapters 12–19), the Son of Man, Jesus the Messiah will return for His Second Coming! Hallelujah!

> Matthew 24:29–31, "Immediately after the tribulation of those days the sun will be darkened, and the moon will not give its light; the stars will fall from heaven, and the powers of the heavens will be shaken. Then the sign of the Son of Man will appear in heaven, and then all the tribes of the earth will mourn, and they will see the Son of Man coming on the clouds of heaven with power and great glory. And He will send His angels with a great sound of a trumpet, and they will gather together His elect from the four winds, from one end of heaven to the other."

In Messiah's Olivet Discourse (Matthew 24-25), He describes the signs of His Second Coming similar to the prophet Joel in his prophecies of this event (Joel 2:30–32). As the "great trump" sounds at the end of the seven-year tribulation period on Yom Kippur, Messiah will return for His Second Coming. The great trump is an idiom that directly correlates to Yom Kippur, the Day of Atonement. We will discover the idioms of the Lord's feasts in more detail in the final chapter. In summary, the "first trump" refers to the Feast of Pentecost (Shavuot), the "last trump" refers to the Feast of Trumpets, and the "great trump" refers to the Feast of Yom Kippur. On God's appointed year on Yom Kippur, the great trump will sound right before Jesus' glorious appearing, and He and the armies of heaven will come from the clouds of heaven with great power and glory (Rev. 19:11–16).

Messiah also states that "all the tribes of the earth will mourn when they see the Son of Man coming for His day of vengeance" (Isa. 61:2). Why will they mourn? The unbelievers on earth will mourn because they will realize that Messiah is coming to battle them on the Earth, including the Antichrist and his kingdom. Then, Messiah will also judge the nations and redeem His chosen people and the Promised Land of Israel. The children of Israel will also mourn because they will understand that Jesus is the Messiah (Matthew 23:39), the King of Israel (John 1:49), and the One whom they have pierced.

> Zechariah 12:10, "And I will pour on the house of David and on the inhabitants of Jerusalem the Spirit of grace and supplication; *Then they will look on Me whom they pierced.* Yes, they will mourn for Him as one mourns for his only son, and grieve for Him as one grieves for a firstborn."

The children of Israel, as a nation, will realize that Jesus is the Messiah whom they have crucified and rejected. At His Second Coming, if a person, Jew or Gentile, is not a believer in Messiah, it will be too late, as His day of vengeance will be at hand. All of mankind will understand that Jesus is the King of Kings and Lord of Lords!

Revelation 19:11–16, "Now I saw heaven opened, and behold, a white horse. And He who sat on him was called Faithful and True, and in righteousness He judges and makes war. His eyes were like a flame of fire, and on His head were many crowns. He had a name written that no one knew except Himself. He was clothed with a robe dipped in blood, and His name is called The Word of God. And the armies in heaven, clothed in fine linen, white and clean, followed Him on white horses. Now out of His mouth goes a sharp sword, that with it He should strike the nations. And He Himself will rule them with a rod of iron. He Himself treads the winepress of the fierceness and wrath of Almighty God. And He has on His robe and on His thigh a name written: KING OF KINGS AND LORD OF LORDS."

In Jesus' supreme and majestic glory, He will return to earth on a white horse to judge and make war with the Antichrist and his kingdom, the false prophet, and the evil nations who oppose Him. The armies in heaven, including the Old Testament saints, the raptured saints, and the tribulation saints, will be following Messiah on white horses and clothed in white linen.

Can you imagine what that day will be like? For the saints who are following Messiah from heaven, it will be unlike any day we could ever imagine! All of mankind's geniuses put together cannot grasp how awesome this spectacular event will be on that glorious day. Without question, Messiah's Second Coming will be an amazing day for the armies in heaven who are coming down with the King of Kings and Lord of Lords!

At Messiah's First Coming, He came as the sacrificial Lamb of the world (Isa. 53), but at His Second Coming, He will return as the conquering Lion of Judah (Revelation 5:5)! Jesus, who is Faithful and True, will come for His vengeance on the Day of Atonement (Yom Kippur). He will fight and destroy the Antichrist and his kingdom, the false prophet, and all apostate nations who oppose Him, because, as the Scriptures tell us, His robe will be "dipped in blood" from His wrath (Isa. 63:1–6, Rev. 19:13–16). Make no mistake, Messiah's Second Coming, the Day of the Lord, is a day of war, death, and redemption for the remnant of Israel.

Zephaniah 1:14–18, "The great day of the Lord is near; It is near and hastens quickly. The noise of the day of the Lord is bitter; There the mighty men shall cry out. That day is a day of wrath, a day of trouble and distress, a day of devastation and desolation, a day of darkness and gloominess, a day of clouds and thick darkness, a day of trumpet and alarm against the fortified cities and against the high towers. "I will bring distress upon men, and they shall walk like blind men, because they have sinned against the Lord; Their blood shall be poured out like dust, and their flesh like refuse." Neither their silver nor their gold shall be able to deliver them in the day of the Lord's wrath; But the whole land shall be devoured by the fire of His jealousy, for He will make speedy riddance of all those who dwell in the land." (Also see Joel 2:1–2)

Joel 2:30–32, "And I will show wonders in the heavens and in the earth: Blood and fire and pillars of smoke. The sun shall be turned into darkness, and the moon into blood, before the coming of the great and awesome day of the Lord. And it shall come to pass that whoever calls on the name of the Lord shall be saved. *For in Mount Zion and in Jerusalem there shall be deliverance, as the Lord has said, among the remnant whom the Lord calls.*" (emphasis mine)

In these sobering prophecies, Zephaniah and Joel describe Messiah's Second Coming as a dark, gloomy, and devastating day of eternal death and destruction for the Antichrist and His kingdom, all unbelievers, and all evil nations. However, the Lord's remnant will be saved!

THE MAJOR BATTLE FRONT

At Messiah's Second Coming, there will be a major battlefront that extends across the length of Israel; From the northern point of the Valley of Jezreel (Megiddo), through Jerusalem, and south through the Valley of Jehoshaphat (Kidron Valley), into the southernmost point in Petra, Jordan (Edom). Keep in mind, the battle front will be approximately 180 miles in length. Now, let us explore the northern point of the major battlefront, the Valley of Jezreel (Megiddo).

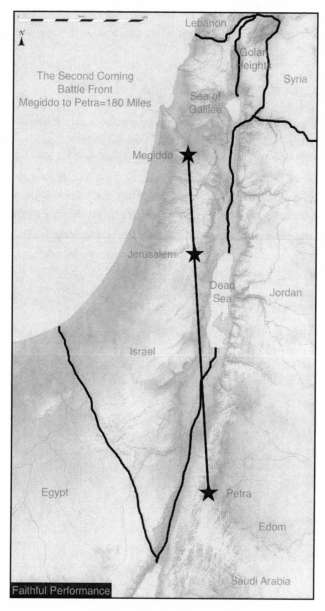

The Second Coming Major Battlefront

THE VALLEY OF JEZREEL, MEGIDDO (ARMAGEDDON)

The most popular and well known battle location at Messiah's Second Coming is the Valley of Jezreel (Megiddo), which is famously referred to as Armageddon (Har-Megiddo-The Mount of Megiddo).

Revelation 16:16, "And they gathered them together to the place called in Hebrew, *Armageddon*."

Armageddon appears only once in the New Testament (Rev. 16:16). The Hebrew word means a mountain or range of hills and a place of crowds (*Strong's Dictionary* #2022, 4023).

During the seven-year tribulation period before Messiah's Second Coming, the Antichrist and his kingdom (ten kings), and other nations, will gather in the Valley of Jezreel for the Battle of Armageddon (Day of the Lord). Throughout history, the Valley of Jezreel has been the battleground for over thirty bloody wars, and it will be the host of the northern battlefront site at Messiah's Second Coming.

In the Old Testament (Tenakh), it records some of the battles that occurred at this notorious site: Deborah and Barak's victory over Sisera (Judg. 4), Gideon's victory over the Midianites (Judg. 7:19-23), King Saul and Jonathan's defeat and death by the Philistines (1 Sam. 31:1-10), King Josiah's defeat and death by Egyptian Pharaoh Necho (2 Chron. 35:20-27), and Jezebel's defeat and violent death, as well (2 Kings 9:30-37). There have been other battles at this site not recorded in the Holy Bible, the most significant being in 1917, when Britain's General Allenby won a decisive battle against the Ottoman Empire (Muslim). As we discovered in the opening chapter, the Balfour Declaration was signed in the Jubilee year of 1917, which was the first official step of the prophetic fulfillment of Israel becoming a nation again in 1948.

The Old Testament battle of King Josiah of Israel and Egyptian Pharaoh Necho gives us a prophetic foreshadow of Messiah's battle in the Valley of Jezreel (Armageddon) at His Second Coming.

2 Chronicles 35:20, "After all this, when Josiah had prepared the temple, Necho king of Egypt came up to fight against Carchemish by the Euphrates; So he came to fight in the Valley of Megiddo (Jezreel)."

In 612 BC, the Babylonian Empire destroyed the Assyrian capital of Nineveh, thus conquering the Assyrian Empire. In 609 BC, the Assyrians reorganized at Carchemish (border of Turkey and Syria), but the Babylonian Empire sent its army to completely destroy them. Pharaoh Necho of Egypt, who was concerned about the Babylonian Empire's rise to power, wanted to reestablish Egypt's world dominance by helping the Assyrians. Pharaoh Necho and the Egyptians marched north from Egypt towards Carchemish to assist the Assyrians in fighting the Babylonians.

As Necho traveled through the southern kingdom of Judah, King Josiah tried to prevent him from passing through at the Valley of Jezreel (Megiddo) and Josiah was killed. The Babylonian Empire eventually defeated Pharaoh Necho and the Assyrians, and they remained the dominant superpower.

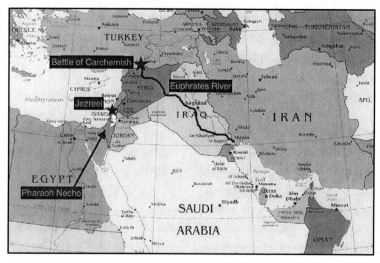

King Josiah and Pharaoh Necho's Battle

Now, with the knowledge of this history and the prophetic foreshadow, let us explore Jeremiah's prophecy about Messiah's Second Coming battle at the Valley of Jezreel. We will begin with the end of the prophecy because it confirms that this prophecy will be fulfilled at the end of the age.

> Jeremiah 46:10–12, "For this is the day of the Lord God of hosts, a day of vengeance, that He may avenge Himself on His adversaries. The sword shall devour; It shall be satiated and made drunk with their blood; For the Lord God of hosts has a sacrifice in the north country by the River Euphrates."

Jeremiah verifies that this prophecy will occur at Messiah's Second Coming when he proclaims, "For this is the day of the Lord God of hosts, a day of vengeance, that He may avenge Himself on His adversaries in the north country by the River Euphrates." As we discovered, the "day of the Lord and the day of vengeance" are eschatological terms for Messiah's Second Coming.

The last part of Jeremiah's prophecy is the exact language used in 2 Chronicles 35:20, "Necho, King of Egypt, came up to fight against Carchemish by the Euphrates; So he came to fight in the Valley of Megiddo" (Jezreel). 2 Chronicles 35:20 gives a prophetic foreshadow of the Valley of Jezreel battle of Jeremiah 46:10–12, because both Scriptures refer to the battle as being "by the River Euphrates." Please note, the Valley of Jezreel is located in the "north country" by the Euphrates River.

As we discussed in previous chapters, oftentimes the Lord prophesied through the current events, and the events shortly thereafter, to give us wisdom, knowledge, and understanding of the ultimate fulfillment of the prophecy at the end of the age. Now, let us explore the beginning of Jeremiah's prophecy.

> Jeremiah 46:1–2, "The word of the Lord which came to Jeremiah the prophet against the nations. Against Egypt.

Concerning the army of Pharaoh Necho, king of Egypt, which was by the River Euphrates in Carchemish."

Jeremiah proclaims an oracle against Egypt by using Pharaoh Necho as a prophetic foreshadow of the Second Coming battle at the Valley of Jezreel. Keep in mind that Jeremiah 46:1–12 is ultimately an end of the age prophecy. Jeremiah continues his oracle by telling us what Egypt's intentions will be at this time in the future.

Jeremiah 46:3–9, "Order the buckler and shield, and draw near to battle! Harness the horses, and mount up, you horsemen! Stand forth with your helmets, polish the spears, put on the armor! Why have I seen them dismayed and turned back? Their mighty ones are beaten down; They have speedily fled, and did not look back, for fear was all around," says the Lord. "Do not let the swift flee away, nor the mighty man escape; *They will stumble and fall toward the north, by the River Euphrates.* "Who is this coming up like a flood, whose waters move like the rivers? Egypt rises up like a flood, and its waters move like the rivers; And he says, 'I will go up and cover the earth, I will destroy the city and its inhabitants.' Come up, O horses, and rage, O chariots! And let the mighty men come forth: *The Ethiopians and the Libyans who handle the shield, and the Lydians who handle and bend the bow.*"

Jeremiah prophesies that the Egyptians, as well as the Ethiopians (Sudan) and Libyans, will rise and travel (flood) toward the north (Megiddo), by the Euphrates River, to battle against the Antichrist. Ancient Ethiopia is modern day Sudan (Cush). Jeremiah declares that "they will stumble and fall toward the north, by the River Euphrates," referring to the Valley of Jezreel (Megiddo). This confirms the prophetic foreshadow of Pharaoh Necho in 2 Chronicles 35:20. The exact scenario will unfold during the tribulation period, as well.

Daniel prophesied about the outcome of this battle as the Antichrist will conquer Egypt, Libya, and Sudan (Ethiopia).

> Daniel 7:24, "The ten horns are ten kings who shall arise from this kingdom. And another shall rise after them; He shall be different from the first ones, a*nd shall subdue three kings.*"

As we discovered, the Antichrist's kingdom will consist of ten kings, and Daniel declares that he will conquer three of the ten kings; Egypt, Libya, and Sudan.

> Daniel 11:40,42–43, "At the time of the end the king of the South shall attack him; and the king of the North shall come against him like a whirlwind, with chariots, horsemen, and with many ships; and he shall enter the countries, overwhelm them, and pass through. *He shall stretch out his hand against the countries, and the land of Egypt shall not escape. He shall have power over the treasures of gold and silver, and over all the precious things of Egypt; also the Libyans and Ethiopians shall follow at his heels.*"

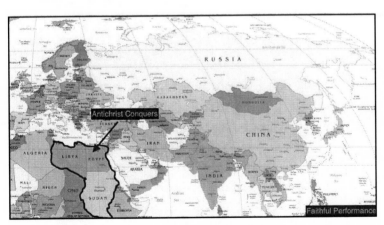

Three Kings the Antichrist Conquers

Daniel confirms Jeremiah's prophecy, as he proclaims that Egypt, the king of the south, will attack the Antichrist, the king of the north, and Egypt will be defeated. He also confirms the three kings that the Antichrist will conquer; Egypt, Libya, and Sudan. Just as the prophetic foreshadow of 2 Chronicles 35:20, this end of the age battle will occur at the famous battlefield in the Valley of Jezreel (Megiddo), Armageddon. As we continue to explore Daniel chapter 11, Daniel also prophesied about the Antichrist's actions after He conquers Egypt, Libya, and Sudan.

Daniel 11:44, "But news from the east and the north shall trouble him; therefore, he shall go out with great fury to destroy and annihilate many."

After the Antichrist conquers Egypt, Libya, and Sudan, he receives troubling news from the east and the north. John also gives us great insight about the Antichrist's troubles, as well.

Revelation 9:14–19, "Saying to the sixth angel who had the trumpet, "Release the four angels who are bound at the great river Euphrates." So the four angels, who had been prepared for the hour and day and month and year, were released to kill a third of mankind. *Now the number of the army of the horsemen was two hundred million; I heard the number of them.* And thus I saw the horses in the vision: those who sat on them had breastplates of fiery red, hyacinth blue, and sulfur yellow; and the heads of the horses were like the heads of lions; and out of their mouths came fire, smoke, and brimstone. *By these three plagues a third of mankind was killed*—by the fire and the smoke and the brimstone which came out of their mouths. For their power is in their mouth and in their tails; for their tails are like serpents, having heads; and with them they do harm."

In John's vision, he describes an army of 200 million that will come from the east and the north to battle against the Antichrist. Although the Antichrist will have influence over the world (Dan. 7:23), prosper and thrive (Dan. 8:24), and do according to his own purpose and will (Dan. 11:36), many nations will fight against him. Just as Egypt, Libya, and Sudan will battle against him, the kings of the east and their 200 million army will also come against him, as well.

In Revelation 16, John also gives us great wisdom concerning the battle at the Valley of Jezreel. He explains that the Euphrates River will be "dried up," so that it can make the way for the kings of the east (200 million) to get to Megiddo (Jezreel). This is the sixth bowl, which precedes the final bowl (seventh bowl), which is Messiah's Second Coming.

> Revelation 16:12–14, 16, "Then the sixth angel poured out his bowl on the great river Euphrates, and its water was dried up, so that the way of the kings from the east might be prepared. And I saw three unclean spirits like frogs coming out of the mouth of the dragon, out of the mouth of the beast, and out of the mouth of the false prophet. *For they are spirits of demons, performing signs, which go out to the kings of the earth and of the whole world, to gather them to the battle of that great day of God Almighty. And they gathered them together to the place called in Hebrew, Armageddon.*" (emphasis mine)

John clearly substantiates the fact that there will be a battle at the Valley of Jezreel (Armageddon), because the Euphrates river will be dried up in order for the kings of the east to travel there. He also states, "the kings of the earth and of the whole world will be gathered to the battle of that great day of God Almighty." All nations will be gathered at the northern point of the battlefront at Messiah's Second Coming, which is the Valley of Jezreel (Megiddo).

Hosea 1:11, "Then the children of Judah and the children of Israel shall be gathered together, and appoint for themselves one head; And they shall come up out of the land, *for great will be the day of Jezree*l!

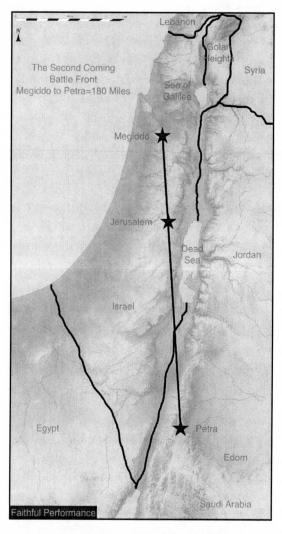

The Major Battlefront of Messiah's Second Coming

THE BATTLE AGAINST JERUSALEM

As we continue along the major battlefront that will occur at the end of the age, there will also be a battle eighty miles south of Megiddo in Jerusalem. At Messiah's Second Coming, the Antichrist and his kingdom and the apostate nations will also be gathered against the holy city Zion (Jerusalem), ready to battle.

> Zechariah 14:1–4, 5, 9, "Behold, the day of the Lord is coming, and your spoil will be divided in your midst. *For I will gather all the nations to battle against Jerusalem*; The city shall be taken, the houses rifled, and the women ravished. Half of the city shall go into captivity, but the remnant of the people shall not be cut off from the city. Then the Lord will go forth and fight against those nations, as He fights in the day of battle. And in that day His feet will stand on the Mount of Olives, which faces Jerusalem on the east (Kidron Valley). And the Mount of Olives shall be split in two, from east to west, making a very large valley; Half of the mountain shall move toward the north and half of it toward the south. Thus the Lord my God will come, and all the saints with You. And the Lord shall be King over all the earth. In that day it shall be— "The Lord is one," and His name one."

At the battle of Jerusalem, Zechariah tells us that the Antichrist, his kingdom, and the evil nations will battle against the holy city, but the Lord Himself will appear at His Second Coming, saving a remnant of the city (Zech. 13:8–9). On that day, Messiah's feet will stand on the Mount of Olives, and from that day forward, He will be King over all the earth and reign for one thousand years (millennial reign)!

> Isaiah 10:20–23, "And it shall come to pass in that day that the remnant of Israel, and such as have escaped of the house

of Jacob, will never again depend on him who defeated them, but will depend on the Lord, the Holy One of Israel, in truth. The remnant will return, the remnant of Jacob, to the Mighty God. For though your people, O Israel, be as the sand of the sea, a remnant of them will return; The destruction decreed shall overflow with righteousness. For the Lord God of hosts will make a determined end in the midst of all the land."

Please note, at the midway point of the tribulation (three and a half years), Messiah warns the children of Israel to flee to the mountains (Matt. 24:15–21) to avoid the great tribulation (last three and a half years). However, at Messiah's Second Coming, He will protect and redeem one-third of the people, His remnant (Zech. 13:8). At that time, Jerusalem will become "a cup of drunkenness to all surrounding nations." Hallelujah!

> Zechariah 12:2–3,6, "Behold, I will make Jerusalem a cup of drunkenness to all the surrounding peoples, when they lay siege against Judah and Jerusalem. And it shall happen in that day that I will make Jerusalem a very heavy stone for all peoples; all who would heave it away will surely be cut in pieces, though all nations of the earth are gathered against it. In that day I will make the governors of Judah like a firepan in the woodpile, and like a fiery torch in the sheaves; they shall devour all the surrounding peoples on the right hand and on the left, but Jerusalem shall be inhabited again in her own place—Jerusalem."

Zechariah prophesies that the Lord will make Jerusalem "a very heavy *stone* that will cut into pieces the nations that are against it." As we discovered in Daniel 2, Messiah is "the stone" that crushes all of the Antichrist's kingdom together at one time.

Daniel 2:34–35, "You watched while a stone was cut out without hands, which struck the image on its feet of iron and clay, and broke them in pieces. *And the stone that struck the image became a great mountain* [kingdom] *and filled the whole earth.*"

Daniel's prophecy directly correlates with Zechariah 12, as Messiah is the stone that will break the Antichrist's kingdom into pieces at His Second Coming. Once Messiah destroys His enemies, His millennial kingdom will become great and fill the earth (millennial reign)!

It is important to understand that there will be two sickles of judgment at Messiah's Second Coming, a sickle of the sword and a sickle of fire (Rev. 2:12, 14:14–20, 19:15). In Zechariah 12:6, he declares "the governors of Judah will be like a firepan in the woodpile, a fiery torch in the sheaves, devouring all of the people surrounding Jerusalem." Zechariah is telling us that at the Battle of Jerusalem, Messiah's enemies will be judged with the sickle of fire. This is not to say that Messiah's sickle of the sword will not come upon them, as well, because it will come upon all nations (Rev. 19:15). The prophets Malachi and John verify the sickle of fire against the Antichrist, his kingdom, and the other nations gathered around Jerusalem.

Malachi 4:1, "For behold, the day is coming, burning like an oven, and all the proud, yes, all who do wickedly will be stubble. *And the day which is coming shall burn them up,*" *says the Lord of hosts,* "That will leave them neither root nor branch."

Revelation 14:17–18, "Then another angel came out of the temple which is in heaven, he also having a sharp sickle. And another angel came out from the altar, *who had power over fire*, and he cried with a loud cry to him who had the sharp sickle, saying, "Thrust in your sharp sickle and gather the clusters of the vine of the earth, for her grapes are fully ripe." (emphasis mine)

If the governors of Judah will be like a "firepan and a fiery torch, burning like an oven" to the enemy nations surrounding Jerusalem, then we can be confident that Malachi and John's prophecies are speaking of the sickle of fire. As we discussed in the previous chapter, could this be speaking of a nuclear weapon?

Zechariah 12:8–11, "In that day the Lord will defend the inhabitants of Jerusalem; the one who is feeble among them in that day shall be like David, and the house of David shall be like God, like the Angel of the Lord before them. It shall be in that day that I will seek to destroy all the nations that come against Jerusalem. And I will pour on the house of David and on the inhabitants of Jerusalem the Spirit of grace and supplication; then they will look on Me whom they pierced. Yes, they will mourn for Him as one mourns for his only son, and grieve for Him as one grieves for a firstborn. *In that day there shall be a great mourning in Jerusalem, like the mourning at Hadad Rimmon in the plain of Megiddo.*"

On the Day of the Lord (Second Coming), He will destroy the Antichrist, his kingdom, the false prophet, and all nations that come against Jerusalem. The remnant will have "the Spirit of grace and supplication poured out on them, and they will also mourn for the One they have pierced." On that day, a great mourning will be in the holy city of Jerusalem like the mourning at Hadad Rimmon (Megiddo). This confirms the prophetic foreshadow discussed at the battlefront of Jezreel, as it is referencing the lamentation for King Josiah, who was mortally wounded at Megiddo (2 Chron. 35:22–25). The middle point of the battlefront at Messiah's Second Coming will be the holy city, Jerusalem.

Micah 2:12–13, "I will surely assemble all of you, O Jacob, I will surely gather the remnant of Israel; I will put them together like sheep of the fold, like a flock in the midst of their pasture; They shall make a loud noise because of so many people. The one who breaks open will come up before them; They will break out, pass through the gate, and go out by it; Their king will pass before them, with the Lord at their head."

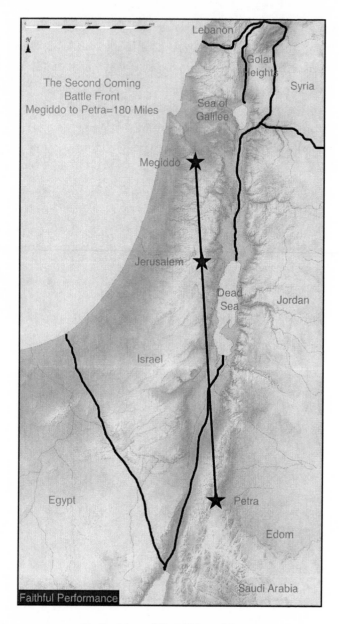

The Battlefront of Messiah's Second Coming

THE VALLEY OF JEHOSHAPHAT

The third location of the 180-mile major battlefront at Messiah's Second Coming is the Valley of Jehoshaphat (Kidron Valley). This famous valley extends north and south in between the Temple Mount and the Mount of Olives in Jerusalem, continuing east through the Judean Desert in the West Bank, to the Jordan Valley. Jehoshaphat means "the Lord has judged" (*Strong's Dictionary* #3092). The Antichrist's kingdom and apostate nations will also be gathered at the Valley of Jehoshaphat!

> Joel 3:1–2, "For behold, in those days and at that time, when I bring back the captives of Judah and Jerusalem, *I will also gather all nations, and bring them down to the Valley of Jehoshaphat*; And I will enter into judgment with them there on account of My people, My heritage Israel, whom they have scattered among the nations." (emphasis mine)

Joel specifically proclaims that Messiah will enter into judgment against all nations at the Valley of Jehoshaphat. It is important to understand that the reason for the Lord's judgment is "on the account of His people and His heritage, Israel." As Joel continues, the Lord prophesies for the nations to prepare for war!

> Joel 3:9–11, "Proclaim this among the nations: "Prepare for war! Wake up the mighty men, let all the men of war draw near, let them come up. Beat your plowshares into swords and your pruning hooks into spears; Let the weak say, 'I am strong.'" Assemble and come, all you nations, and gather together all around. Cause Your mighty ones to go down there, O Lord."

In 2 Chronicles 20, we find a prophetic foreshadow of the battle at the Valley of Jehoshaphat, which will occur at Messiah's Second Coming. King Jehoshaphat of Judah was warned that the people of Moab, Ammon, Mount Seir, and others, were coming to battle against Jerusalem. Jehoshaphat proclaimed a fast throughout the kingdom of Judah for the children of Israel to seek the Lord and ask for His deliverance (2 Chron. 20:3–4). As Jehoshaphat and the kingdom of Judah came together, fasting and praying, Jehoshaphat called upon the Lord for His help and deliverance (2 Chron. 20:5–12). As Jehoshaphat's prayer ended, and all of the kingdom of Judah stood before the Lord (2 Chron. 20:3), the Holy Spirit came upon Jahaziel, a Levite priest.

> 2 Chronicles 20:15, 17, "And he said, "Listen, all you of Judah and you inhabitants of Jerusalem, and you, King Jehoshaphat! Thus says the Lord to you: 'Do not be afraid nor dismayed because of this great multitude, for the battle is not yours, but God's. Tomorrow go down against them. They will surely come up by the Ascent of Ziz, and you will find them at the end of the brook before the Wilderness of Jeruel (a "desert" on the ascent from the valley of the Dead Sea towards Jerusalem). *You will not need to fight in this battle. Position yourselves, stand still and see the salvation of the Lord, who is with you, O Judah and Jerusalem!'* Do not fear or be dismayed; tomorrow go out against them, for the Lord is with you."

King Jehoshaphat was told by the Levite Jahaziel that the kingdom of Judah would not need to fight in the battle because it was God's battle! The Almighty fought this battle, "*on the account of His people, His heritage, Israel.*" This is a prophetic foreshadow of Messiah's Second Coming battle at the Valley of Jehoshaphat prophesied in Joel 3:1–2, as He will fight, "*on account of My people, My heritage Israel.*" The conclusion of Jehoshaphat's battle gives us great insight as to what will occur at Messiah's battle in the Valley of Jehoshaphat at His Second Coming.

2 Chronicles 20:22–24, "Now when they began to sing and to praise, *the Lord set ambushes against the people of Ammon, Moab, and Mount Seir, who had come against Judah; and they were defeated.* For the people of Ammon and Moab stood up against the inhabitants of Mount Seir to utterly kill and destroy them. And when they had made an end of the inhabitants of Seir, *they helped to destroy one another.* So when Judah came to a place overlooking the wilderness, they looked toward the multitude; and there were their dead bodies, fallen on the earth. No one had escaped." (emphasis mine)

When the kingdom of Judah praised and sang to the Lord, He set ambushes against the Ammonites, Moabites, and others, turning one against the other, totally destroying them. Just as the Lord redeemed King Jehoshaphat and the kingdom of Judah, when the remnant of Israel praises and calls out to Messiah, He will also deliver and redeem them, as well!

Matthew 23:39, "For I say to you, you shall see Me no more till you say, 'Blessed is He who comes in the name of the Lord!'"

Daniel also gives us knowledge about the prophetic foreshadow of the battle at the Valley of Jehoshaphat.

Daniel 11:41, "He shall also enter the Glorious Land, and many countries shall be overthrown; *but these shall escape from his hand: Edom, Moab, and the prominent people of Ammon.*"

Although Edom, Moab, and the people of Ammon escape from being conquered by the Antichrist, they will wage war against the children of Israel at the end of the age. Edom (Saudi Arabia), is where the Moabites, Ammonites, and the people of Seir are located. As we discovered in the previous chapter, Edom (Saudi Arabia) will be destroyed by the sickle of the sword and the sickle of fire. At Messiah's Second Coming, He will also judge Moab, Ammon, and Mount Seir, as well (Isa. 15, 16, 21; Jer. 49; Ezek. 35).

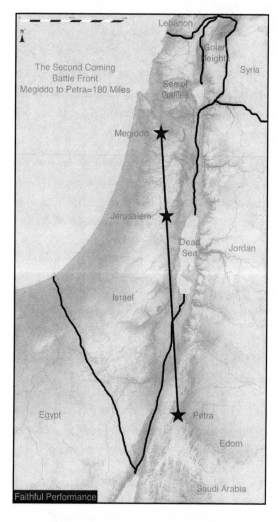

The Major Battlefront at Messiah's Second Coming

In a prophetic foreshadow, as King Jehoshaphat's battle concluded, the Lord turned his enemies against one another until they were all destroyed. At Messiah's Second Coming, He will also confuse the nations and their horses at the battle in the Valley of Jehoshaphat!

> Zechariah 12:4, "In that day," says the Lord, "I will strike every horse with confusion, and its rider with madness; I will open My eyes on the house of Judah, and will strike every horse of the peoples with blindness."

The Valley of Jehoshaphat is named after King Jehoshaphat, because the valley is where the Lord fought "on account of Jehoshaphat and the kingdom of Judah." At Messiah's Second Coming, He will "enter into judgment on the account of His people, His heritage, Israel" in the Valley of Jehoshaphat, as well!

> Joel 3:12–17, "Let the nations be wakened, and come up to the Valley of Jehoshaphat; For there I will sit to judge all the surrounding nations. Put in the sickle, for the harvest is ripe. Come, go down; For the winepress is full, The vats overflow— For their wickedness is great." *Multitudes, multitudes in the valley of decision! For the day of the Lord is near in the valley of decision.* The sun and moon will grow dark, and the stars will diminish their brightness. The Lord also will roar from Zion, and utter His voice from Jerusalem; The heavens and earth will shake; But the Lord will be a shelter for His people, and the strength of the children of Israel. "So you shall know that I am the Lord your God, dwelling in Zion My holy mountain. Then Jerusalem shall be holy, and no aliens shall ever pass through her again." (Also see Joel 3:1–2; Matt. 25)

As the nations and multitudes of people are gathered in the Valley of Jehoshaphat (valley of decision), Messiah will put in His sickle, as the harvest will be ripe, separating sheep nations from goat nations (Matt. 25). Joel describes the Day of the Lord as "the sun and moon will grow dark, the stars will diminish their brightness," which is identical to Messiah's description of His Second Coming (Matt. 24:29–31). John describes Messiah's judgment in Joel 3 in the exact same manner.

> Revelation 14:14–16, "Then I looked, and behold, a white cloud, and on the cloud sat One like the Son of Man, having on His head a golden crown, and in His hand a sharp sickle. And another angel came out of the temple, crying with a loud voice to Him who sat on the cloud, *"Thrust in Your sickle and reap, for the time has come for You to reap, for the harvest of the earth is ripe."* So He who sat on the cloud thrust in His sickle on the earth, and the earth was reaped."* (emphasis mine)

Just as the fear of God was upon all of the kingdoms after the battle during Jehoshaphat's day, all of the kingdoms of the world will have the fear of God in them during Messiah's Second Coming and millennial reign! The kingdom of Judah and Israel will also enjoy rest from all around, just as God delivered for Jehoshaphat and Judah.

> 2 Chronicles 20:29–30, "And the fear of God was on all the kingdoms of those countries when they heard that the Lord had fought against the enemies of Israel. Then the realm of Jehoshaphat was quiet, for his God gave him rest all around."

> Revelation 19:15, "Now out of His mouth goes a sharp sword, that with it He should strike the nations. And He Himself will rule them with a rod of iron." (Also see Ps. 2:9; Rev. 2:27).

THE MAJOR BATTLEFRONT DESTROYED

The major battlefront at Messiah's Second Coming will completely manifest during the tribulation period, and will expand over the area that stretches from the Valley of Jezreel (Megiddo), through Jerusalem, and southward through the Valley of Jehoshaphat onto Petra, Jordan (Edom). Why does the battlefront continue to stretch into Petra, Jordan? Remember, at the midpoint of the tribulation (three and a half years), when the Antichrist causes the abomination of desolation, Messiah commands the children of Israel to "flee to the mountains."

> Matthew 24:15-16,21, "Therefore when you see the 'abomination of desolation,' spoken of by Daniel the prophet, standing in the holy place" (whoever reads, let him understand), *"then let those who are in Judea flee to the mountains. For then there will be great tribulation, such as has not been since the beginning of the world until this time, no, nor ever shall be."* (Also see Rev. 12:6,14)

The widely held belief among Bible scholars and prophecy teachers is that the children of Israel who flee from the Antichrist's persecution will travel to Petra, Jordan (Edom). They will remain there for the duration of the great tribulation, the last three and a half years of the age. Petra is a city that is "cut out" of the mountainside in Jordan. It is well known for its rock-cut architecture and water conduit system, so it is a perfect shelter and safe haven for God's elect during this horrific time period. Isaiah gives us great insight of the battlefront extending to Petra (Edom).

> Isaiah 34:1-6, "Come near, you nations, to hear, and heed, you people! Let the earth hear, and all that is in it, the world and all things that come forth from it. For the indignation of the Lord is against all nations, and His fury against all their

armies; He has utterly destroyed them, He has given them over to the slaughter. Also their slain shall be thrown out; Their stench shall rise from their corpses, and the mountains shall be melted with their blood. All the host of heaven shall be dissolved, and the heavens shall be rolled up like a scroll; All their host shall fall down as the leaf falls from the vine, and as fruit falling from a fig tree." *For My sword shall be bathed in heaven; Indeed, it shall come down on Edom, and on the people of My curse, for judgment.* The sword of the Lord is filled with blood, it is made overflowing with fatness, with the blood of lambs and goats, with the fat of the kidneys of rams. *For the Lord has a sacrifice in Bozrah, and a great slaughter in the land of Edom."* (Also see Isa. 63:1-6; Jer. 49:13)

Isaiah is prophesying of Messiah's Second Coming, His day of vengeance, as he describes the judgment on Edom and Bozrah. As we discovered, Edom is a region of land in Jordan and Saudi Arabia. Messiah will pour out His judgment on Edom and Bozrah, while the children of Israel are secured in Petra. Please note, at Messiah's Second Coming, Judah will be saved first!

Zechariah 12:7–9, "The Lord will save the tents of Judah first, so that the glory of the house of David and the glory of the inhabitants of Jerusalem shall not become greater than that of Judah."

What makes Messiah's Second Coming even more interesting is that two other divine judgments from the Lord occurred in the Valley of Jehoshaphat (Jordan Valley), as well. In Noah's day, it is believed that they built the ark in the Jordan Valley. The Jordan Valley is near the Dead Sea (Valley of Jehoshaphat) and all of the people on earth, except for Noah and his family, died there during the Great Flood (Gen. 8:21–24). Sodom and Gomorrah was also located in the Jordan Valley, just north of the Dead Sea

(Valley of Jehoshaphat), and it was destroyed by the sickle of fire (Gen. 8:21-24).

The book of Luke gives us great insight and confirmation that these two events are a double prophetic foreshadow of Messiah's third judgment at the Valley of Jehoshaphat at His Second Coming.

Luke 17:26–30, *"And as it was in the days of Noah, so it will be also in the days of the Son of Man*: They ate, they drank, they married wives, they were given in marriage, until the day that Noah entered the ark, and the flood came and destroyed them all. *Likewise, as it was also in the days of Lot*: They ate, they drank, they bought, they sold, they planted, they built; but on the day that Lot went out of Sodom *it rained fire and brimstone from heaven and destroyed them all. Even so will it be in the day when the Son of Man is revealed."*

Messiah specifically describes the days of Noah and the days of Lot as prophetic foreshadows to what will occur at His Second Coming. The Lord will definitely pour out his divine judgment for the third time at the Valley of Jehoshaphat!

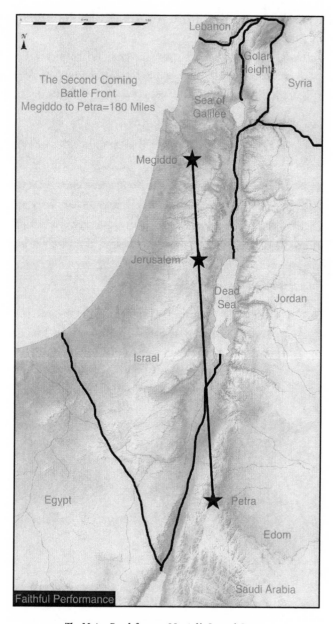

The Major Battlefront at Messiah's Second Coming

As we discovered, the major battlefront at Messiah's Second Coming will be located from the Valley of Jehoshaphat, including the area of Petra (Edom, Bozrah), and will extend through Jerusalem to the Valley of Jezreel (Megiddo). The distance between these battleground sites are approximately 180 miles. The distance from Megiddo to Jerusalem is approximately 80 miles, and from Jerusalem to Petra is approximately 100 miles, for a total of approximately 180 miles. Is the distance of the major battlefront prophesied in the Holy Bible?

Revelation 14:20, "And the winepress was trampled outside the city, and blood came out of the winepress, up to the horses' bridles, for one thousand six hundred furlongs."

John prophesies that Messiah's winepress will produce so much blood that it will come up to the horses' bridle, which is approximately four feet high. He also declares that it will be 1,600 furlongs in length, which is approximately 180 miles! This is incredible! John confirms that Messiah's Second Coming battlefront will be from Megiddo to Petra.

Many Bible scholars and prophecy teachers have debated the interpretation of the blood coming up to the horses' bridle, because it would take trillions upon trillions of lives to produce enough blood to come up four feet high and expand 180 miles in length. Also, experts have estimated that the total number of people who will die at Messiah's Second Coming is approximately 500 million. Although that is a tremendous amount of people, it is not nearly enough to fulfill John's prophecy. So how will the blood come up four feet high for 180 miles? Let us review the sixth bowl judgment of the great tribulation.

Revelation 16:21, "And great hail from heaven fell upon men, each hailstone about the weight of a talent."

Before Messiah returns to Earth (seventh bowl judgment), the sixth bowl judgment will pour out great hail from heaven. Each piece of hail will weigh approximately 60–100 pounds! So, when Messiah comes for His day of vengeance at the seventh bowl, great hail and death will have come over approximately 500 million people. As each piece of hail melts and mixes with the blood of the slain, the water infused blood could easily come up four feet high and 180 miles long.

Can you imagine what the Day of the Lord will be like as approximately 500 million people are thrown into the winepress of Messiah, causing the blood to flow up four feet high for 180 miles? Certainly, it is safe to say that all of mankind should want to be included in Messiah's armies who will be coming from heaven (Rev. 19:14). The Holy Bible clearly tells us that Messiah's Second Coming will be a day of death and destruction for unbelievers, and that there will be a river of blood four feet high from Megiddo to Petra!

Now, it is important to understand that there are two different sickles that describe Messiah's winepress, one of the sword and the other of fire.

> Revelation 14:14–20, "Then I looked, and behold, a white cloud, and on the cloud sat One like the Son of Man, having on His head a golden crown, and in His hand a sharp sickle. And another angel came out of the temple, crying with a loud voice to Him who sat on the cloud, "Thrust in Your sickle and reap, for the time has come for You to reap, for the harvest of the earth is ripe." So He who sat on the cloud thrust in His sickle on the earth, and the earth was reaped. Then another angel came out of the temple which is in heaven, he also having a sharp sickle. And another angel came out from the altar, who had power over fire, and he cried with a loud cry to him who had the sharp sickle, saying, "Thrust in your sharp sickle and gather the clusters of the vine of the earth, for her grapes are fully ripe." So the angel thrust his sickle into the earth and gathered the vine of the earth, and threw it into the great winepress of the wrath of God."

Just as John prophesies, there will be a sickle of the sword and a sickle of fire, as we have discovered both in this chapter. Messiah's sickle of the sword will kill the evil nations and people, staining His robe (Isa. 63:1–6; Rev. 19:13), and the sickle of fire will destroy the people and the land of the evil nations (Isa. 34:1–8; Jer. 49:17; Zech. 12:2–3, 6). Both sickles of judgment have the same fatal result, the winepress of Messiah! Ezekiel also confirms the sickle of the sword and the sickle of fire.

Ezekiel 38:19,21–22, "For in My jealousy and in the fire of My wrath I have spoken: 'Surely in that day there shall be a great earthquake in the land of Israel, *I will call for a sword against Gog throughout all My mountains," says the Lord God. "Every man's sword will be against his brother. And I will bring him to judgment with pestilence and bloodshed; I will rain down on him, on his troops, and on the many peoples who are with him, flooding rain, great hailstones, fire, and brimstone."* (emphasis mine)

Ezekiel prophesies that every man's sword will be against his brother, which verifies the sickle of the sword. He also states that the Lord will send fire and brimstone on the nations, as well, also verifying the sickle of fire. Zechariah prophesies about the affects of the sickle of fire at Messiah's Second Coming.

Zechariah 14:12, "And this shall be the plague with which the Lord will strike all the people who fought against Jerusalem: Their flesh shall dissolve while they stand on their feet, their eyes shall dissolve in their sockets, and their tongues shall dissolve in their mouths."

Zechariah describes the affects of the angel's sickle of fire, which are similar to the affects of a nuclear weapon, as flesh, eyes, and tongue are dissolved in this manner. In any case, this will be a horrific event, as it is the day of the Lord's vengeance, His Second Coming!

> Isaiah 66:15–16, "For behold, the Lord will come with fire and with His chariots, like a whirlwind, to render His anger with fury, and His rebuke with flames of fire. *For by fire and by His sword the Lord will judge all flesh; And the slain of the Lord shall be many.*"

In conclusion, the Second Coming is a battle between God versus Satan, Messiah against the Antichrist, Isaac's descendants versus Ishmael's, and Jacobs' (Israel) descendants against Esau's (Edom). Of course, all nations of the world will be gathered at the major battlefront in the Day of the Lord, but the primary nations will be Israel's historical enemies, which are today Islamic Muslim nations. Remember, God "declares the end from the beginning, and from ancient times things that are not yet done" (Isa. 46:10). Messiah will summon the Antichrist, his kingdom, and all of the evil nations to the major battlefront. The battlefront will extend from the northern point of the Valley of Jezreel in Megiddo, through Jerusalem and the Valley of Jehoshaphat (Kidron Valley), and unto the southernmost point in Petra, Jordan.

The Second Coming is the Day of the Lord, the Day of Atonement (Yom Kippur) for the nation of Israel (remnant), and His day of vengeance on the Antichrist, his kingdom, the false prophet, and the evil nations. Messiah's day of vengeance will be a day like no other in history, as He will pour out His wrath and destruction. After His day of vengeance has concluded, the Antichrist and the false prophet will be captured and thrown alive into the lake of fire burning with brimstone!

> Revelation 19:19–21, "And I saw the beast, the kings of the earth, and their armies, gathered together to make war against Him who sat on the horse and against His army.

Then the beast was captured, and with him the false prophet who worked signs in his presence, by which he deceived those who received the mark of the beast and those who worshiped his image. *These two were cast alive into the lake of fire burning with brimstone.* And the rest were killed with the sword which proceeded from the mouth of Him who sat on the horse."

Messiah will destroy all of the nations and people who oppose Him, and both the Antichrist and the false prophet will be thrown alive into the lake of fire. The remaining evil people and nations, whose flesh isn't dissolved by the Lord's plague (sickle of fire), will be killed by His sword (sickle of the sword). After the Lord pours out His wrath and vengeance on Yom Kippur, a great supper will take place!

> Revelation 19:17–18, 21, "Then I saw an angel standing in the sun; and he cried with a loud voice, saying to all the birds that fly in the midst of heaven, "Come and gather together for the supper of the great God, that you may eat the flesh of kings, the flesh of captains, the flesh of mighty men, the flesh of horses and of those who sit on them, and the flesh of all people, free and slave, both small and great. And all the birds were filled with their flesh."

The great supper of the Lord for the birds and the beasts is also prophesied in Ezekiel 39:17–20. Once Messiah destroys the Antichrist, his kingdom, the evil nations, and casts the Antichrist and the false prophet alive into the lake of fire, the birds of the air and the beasts of the field will fill themselves with the flesh of the people who fought against Messiah. After the Lord's great supper for the animals, the prophet Ezekiel gives us insight as to the amount of people that will be slain, and he tells us how their remains will be buried.

Ezekiel 39:12–16, "It will come to pass in that day that I will give Gog a burial place there in Israel, the valley of those who pass by east of the sea; and it will obstruct travelers, because there they will bury Gog and all his multitude. Therefore, they will call it the Valley of Hamon Gog. *For seven months the house of Israel will be burying them, in order to cleanse the land.* Indeed, all the people of the land will be burying, and they will gain renown for it on the day that I am glorified," says the Lord God. "They will set apart men regularly employed, with the help of a search party, to pass through the land and bury those bodies remaining on the ground, in order to cleanse it. At the end of seven months they will make a search. The search party will pass through the land; and when anyone sees a man's bone, he shall set up a marker by it, till the buriers have buried it in the Valley of Hamon Gog. The name of the city will also be Hamonah. Thus they shall cleanse the land.'"

Ezekiel declares that it will take seven months to bury the winepress of God after Messiah's Second Coming. There will be approximately 500 million people who will die at Messiah's victory. Even so, travelers will be detoured from the Valley of Hamon-Gog because there will be hundreds of millions of bodies. The burial event will take place during the first seven months of Messiah's one-thousand-year reign on earth (millennial reign). According to the Torah (Num. 19), and as Ezekiel prophesied, the bones are buried so that the land is cleansed from the defilement of the dead bodies. At the Lord's great supper for the birds and the beasts, they will help dispose of the flesh; however, the bones will need to be buried for the land to be cleansed.

Joel 3:18,20–21, "And it will come to pass in that day that the mountains shall drip with new wine, the hills shall flow with milk, and all the brooks of Judah shall be flooded with water; A fountain shall flow from the house of the Lord and water the Valley of Acacias. Judah shall abide forever, and Jerusalem from generation to generation. For I will acquit them of the guilt of bloodshed, whom I had not acquitted; For the Lord dwells in Zion."

In this beautiful and encouraging prophecy, Joel confirms Israel's redemption (remnant) at His Second Coming (Yom Kippur). The Valley of Acacias is a historical place commonly associated with both victory and failure. It is located on the eastern side of the Jordan River and north of the Dead Sea. Joel tells us that the water from the house of the Lord will flow down to the Valley of Acacias. This is symbolic of God's grace and forgiveness of the kingdoms of Israel and Judah, as He will acquit their guilt of bloodshed. On the Day of Atonement (Yom Kippur), Messiah's Second Coming, He will redeem and cover the nation of Israel with victory and begin His millennial reign!

Zephaniah 3:14–20, "Sing, O daughter of Zion! Shout, O Israel! Be glad and rejoice with all your heart, O daughter of Jerusalem! The Lord has taken away your judgments he has cast out your enemy. The King of Israel, the Lord, is in your midst; You shall see disaster no more. In that day it shall be said to Jerusalem: "Do not fear; Zion, let not your hands be weak. The Lord your God is in your midst, The Mighty One, will save; He will rejoice over you with gladness, He will quiet you with His love, He will rejoice over you with singing." "I will gather those who sorrow over the appointed assembly, Who are among you, to whom its reproach is a burden. Behold, at that time I will deal with all who afflict you; I will save the lame, and gather those who were driven out; I will appoint them for praise and fame in every land where they were put to shame. At that time, I will bring you back, even at the time I gather you; For I will give you fame and praise among all the peoples of the earth, when I return your captives before your eyes," Says the Lord."

CHAPTER 10

MESSIAH'S MILLENNIAL KINGDOM

After Messiah's incredible victory at His Second Coming, He will set up His kingdom on David's everlasting throne in Jerusalem for His millennial reign! He will rule the nations from Jerusalem (Zion) as the King of Israel for one thousand years, and fulfill all of the everlasting covenants and prophecies in the Holy Bible (Matt. 5:17–18). As the Antichrist and the false prophet will be cast alive into the lake of fire at Messiah's Second Coming (Rev. 19:20), Satan will be "chained and bound" during Messiah's millennial reign.

> Revelation 20:1–3, "Then I saw an angel coming down from heaven, having the key to the bottomless pit and a great chain in his hand. *He laid hold of the dragon, that serpent of old, who is the Devil and Satan, and bound him for a thousand years*; and he cast him into the bottomless pit, and shut him up, and set a seal on him, so that he should deceive the nations no more till the thousand years were finished. But after these things he must be released for a little while." (emphasis mine)

John prophesies that the serpent of old, Satan, will be bound during Messiah's millennial reign on earth. Nevertheless, after the thousand years expire, the Lord will release him for a short time, as we will discuss later. The prophet Daniel also verifies that Messiah will set up His millennial kingdom on earth after His Second Coming.

> Daniel 7:13–14, "I was watching in the night visions, and behold, One like the Son of Man, coming with the clouds of heaven (Second Coming)! He came to the Ancient of Days, and they brought Him near before Him. *Then to Him was given dominion and glory and a kingdom, that all peoples, nations, and languages should serve Him. His dominion is an everlasting dominion, which shall not pass away, and His kingdom the one which shall not be destroyed.*" (emphasis mine)

As we discovered in the previous chapters, Daniel 7 prophesies about four kingdoms that will rise to power at the end of the age (Babylonian, Medo-Persian, Grecian, and the Antichrist's kingdom). In the very next paragraph, Daniel describes the Ancient of Days (God Almighty) and declares that the beast, the Antichrist and his kingdom, will be thrown into the lake of fire (Dan. 7:11–12; Rev. 19:20). He also tells us that Messiah descends from the clouds of heaven (Second Coming), and He will have dominion and glory over all nations during His earthly kingdom. Daniel also confirms that all people, nations, and languages will serve Messiah during the millennial reign.

> Daniel 2:44, "And in the days of these kings the God of heaven will set up a kingdom which shall never be destroyed; and the kingdom shall not be left to other people; it shall break in pieces and consume all these kingdoms, and it shall stand forever." (Also see Dan. 7:14, 28)

Daniel proclaims that Messiah will set up His kingdom on earth in the days of these kings, which is at His Second Coming. The word *kings* refers to the Antichrist kingdom's ten kings (Babylonian,

Medo-Persian, Grecian Empire's conglomerate land area). He declares that Messiah will break into pieces and consume all of these kingdoms, and His kingdom will stand forever!

> Daniel 2:35, "Then the iron, the clay, the bronze, the silver, and the gold *were crushed together*, and became like chaff from the summer threshing floors; the wind carried them away so that no trace of them was found. *And the stone that struck the image became a great mountain and filled the whole earth.*" (emphasis mine)

As we discovered in the previous chapters, at Messiah's Second Coming, Messiah (stone) will crush the Antichrist's kingdom, which includes the Babylonian, Medo-Persian, and Grecian Empires. Afterwards, Messiah (stone) will become a great kingdom (mountain)! Messiah also prophesied about His millennial kingdom on earth and commanded us to pray for it.

> Matthew 6:9–10, "In this manner, therefore, pray: Our Father in heaven, hallowed be Your name. *Your kingdom come. Your will be done on earth as it is in heaven.*" (emphasis mine)

Christians have recited the Lord's prayer millions of times throughout history. It is a prayer that Messiah commanded us to pray. Yet, do we really understand the true meaning of, "Your kingdom come, Your will be done, on earth as it is in heaven?"

The Lord's prayer is a prophetic calling to Messiah to come and establish His millennial kingdom on earth! When we pray, "Our Father in heaven, hallowed be Your name," we are giving honor and glory to the King of Kings and Lord of Lords, Jesus. When we pray, "Your kingdom come, Your will be done, on earth as it is in heaven," we are acknowledging the Lord's righteous sovereignty over the universe, thus waiting and anticipating His millennial kingdom to be established on Earth as it is in heaven. One of the reasons for this prayer, if not the main reason, is to pray for His millennial kingdom on Earth! The prophet Zechariah prophesies about this glorious, amazing time in the future.

> Zechariah 14:9, "And the Lord shall be King over all the earth. In that day it shall be, "The Lord is one," and His name one."

Why does Messiah rule for one thousand years on Earth after His Second Coming? What would be the point after He has destroyed the Antichrist, his kingdom, and all evil nations? Let us remember, according to the Holy Bible, Messiah has to fulfill "every jot and tittle" of the Torah and the prophets.

> Matthew 5:17–18, "Do not think that I came to destroy the Torah or the Prophets. I did not come to destroy but to fulfill. For assuredly, I say to you, till heaven and earth pass away, one jot or one tittle will by no means pass from the Torah till all is fulfilled."

THE FULFILLMENT OF THE EVERLASTING COVENANTS

Messiah prophesies that He will fulfill *all* of the Torah and the prophets, including the promises of the Abrahamic, Davidic, and New Covenants. During His millennial reign, Messiah will fulfill the everlasting promises to the House of Israel and Judah. In summary, in the Abrahamic Covenant, God promised Abraham that through his pure royal lineage seed (Isaac, Jacob, and their descendants), the Seed of Israel (Messiah) would come through him (Gen. 12:3). The promise was made by God alone, as it was a unilateral, unconditional, irrevocable, and everlasting covenant with Abraham and his descendants (Israel). God also confirmed His promise to Abraham by "walking down the marriage aisle" between the pieces of animals to confirm the sworn oath (Gen. 15:8–17). In the Abrahamic Covenant, God also promised the children of Israel a specific piece of land, the Promised Land of Canaan, which today is partially located in Israel (Gen. 13:14; 15:18–21). It is important to understand that the "pure royal lineage descendants" (the children of Israel) have never occupied *all* of the Promised Land of Canaan, but they will receive their inheritance at Messiah's millennial reign. As God promised, He will fulfill!

Hebrews 11:8–9, *"By faith Abraham obeyed when he was called to go out to the place which he would receive as an inheritance.* And he went out, not knowing where he was going. By faith he dwelt in the land of promise as in a foreign country, dwelling in tents with Isaac and Jacob, the heirs with him of the same promise." (emphasis mine)

During Messiah's millennial kingdom, He will also fulfill the unilateral, unconditional, irrevocable, and everlasting promise made to David, the Davidic Covenant.

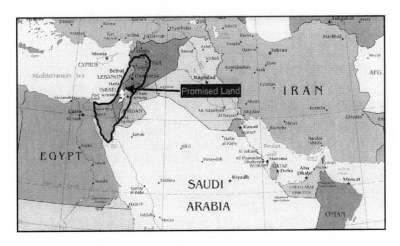

Promised Land-Free map from biblesnet.com

Luke 1:31–33, "And behold, you will conceive in your womb and bring forth a Son, and shall call His name Jesus. He will be great, and will be called the Son of the Highest; *and the Lord God will give Him the throne of His father David. And He will reign over the house of Jacob forever, and of His kingdom there will be no end."* (emphasis mine)

The Davidic Covenant builds upon the Abrahamic Covenant, as it also prophesies that Jesus will rule from David's everlasting throne as King during His thousand-year reign on Earth (2 Sam. 7:10–14, 16). At the beginning of the Davidic Covenant prophecy, the prophet Nathan confirmed the Abrahamic Covenant when he told David that God had appointed a specific place for His people, which is the Promised Land of Canaan. God also promised David a "Seed" who would become King and thereby establish His eternal kingdom on David's throne. This prophecy could not be speaking of Solomon because his kingdom was divided after his death (1 Kings 12). Jesus fulfilled the "Seed" prophecy as Joseph and Mary's genealogy (both direct descendants of David) call him the Son of Abraham and the Son of David (Matt. 1, Luke 3). This clearly confirms Jesus' earthly lineage through the Abrahamic and Davidic Covenants. David also prophetically wrote in Psalms that Jesus is his Lord!

Psalm 110:1–2, "The Lord (God) said to my Lord (Jesus), "Sit at My right hand, till I make Your enemies Your footstool." The Lord shall send the rod of Your strength out of Zion. Rule in the midst of Your enemies!"

Just as God's other prophets did, David understood the future birth of Jesus the Messiah, and how He would establish David's throne in Zion (Jerusalem) at His millennial reign!

Isaiah 9:6–7, "For unto us a Child is born, unto us a Son is given; And the government will be upon His shoulder.

And His name will be called Wonderful, Counselor, Mighty God, Everlasting Father, Prince of Peace. *Of the increase of His government and peace there will be no end, upon the throne of David and over His kingdom, to order it and establish it with judgment and justice from that time forward, even forever. The zeal of the Lord of hosts will perform this."* (emphasis mine)

As our world today experiences corruption, injustice, and fraud in our governments, Isaiah prophesies that Jesus will establish His kingdom with righteous judgment, justice, and peace, forever and ever! This will begin at His millennial reign on Earth after His Second Coming. The world's governments will be centered around the holy city, Jerusalem, and Messiah will rule the world from David's throne!

Psalms 2:1–9, "Why do the nations rage, and the people plot a vain thing? The kings of the earth set themselves, and the rulers take counsel together, against the Lord and against His anointed, saying, "Let us break their bonds in pieces and cast away their cords from us." He who sits in the heavens shall laugh; The Lord shall hold them in derision. Then He shall speak to them in His wrath, and distress them in His deep displeasure: "Yet I have set My King on My holy hill of Zion." "I will declare the decree: *The Lord has said to Me, 'You are My Son, today I have begotten You. Ask of Me, and I will give You the nations for Your inheritance, and the ends of the earth for Your possession. You shall break them with a rod of iron; You shall dash them to pieces like a potter's vessel.'*"

When we look around our broken world today, all believers should be praying and yearning for an earthly messianic kingdom of peace, justice, and righteous judgment. Our prayers will be completely fulfilled at Messiah's earthly millennial kingdom and He will rule with a rod of iron!

Isaiah 32:16–18, "Then justice will dwell in the wilderness, and righteousness remains in the fruitful field. The work of righteousness will be peace, and the effect of righteousness, quietness and assurance forever. My people will dwell in a peaceful habitation, in secure dwellings, and in quiet resting places." (Also see Isaiah 42:3–4)

Isaiah 61:8, 11, "For I, the Lord, love justice; I hate robbery for burnt offering; I will direct their work in truth, and will make with them an *everlasting covenant*. For as the earth brings forth its bud, as the garden causes the things that are sown in it to spring forth, so the Lord God will cause righteousness and praise to spring forth before all the nations."

The final covenant, the New Covenant, will also be completely fulfilled at Messiah's millennial reign, as well. In summary, the New Covenant is a unilateral, unconditional, irrevocable, and everlasting covenant with the House of Israel and Judah (Jer. 31:31–40). The covenant states that the Lord will "put His law in their minds and write it on their hearts, so that He will be their God and they shall be His people" (Jer. 31:31–40). This will occur during the tribulation period and will continue through the Second Coming and millennial kingdom. Please note, the New Covenant fulfills the Abrahamic Covenant (Jer. 31:38–40) and the Davidic Covenant (Jer. 31:33), as Jesus is the Seed of Israel and will be their King during this time, and forevermore.

The children of Israel will also inherit *all* of the Promised Land of Canaan during the millennial reign, as promised in the everlasting covenants. Without question, at Messiah's millennial kingdom, He will rule the Earth on David's everlasting throne in Zion (Jerusalem) as King of Israel, fulfilling the Abrahamic, the Davidic, and the New Covenants. What a glorious and incredible time this will be for believers who dwell in Jerusalem (Zion) for Messiah's millennial kingdom!

Joel 3:21, "The LORD dwells in Zion!"

MESSIAH'S JEWISH KINGDOM

Will Messiah's millennial kingdom be a restored Jewish kingdom? God's messenger, the angel Gabriel, confirms Jesus' earthly reign for one-thousand years over the House of Israel and Judah (Jewish) on David's throne (Jewish). He also confirms that Messiah's kingdom will continue into eternity, forever and ever!

> Luke 1:31–33, "And behold, you will conceive in your womb and bring forth a Son, and shall call His name Jesus. He will be great, and will be called the Son of the Highest; *and the Lord God will give Him the throne of His father David. And He will reign over the house of Jacob forever, and of His kingdom there will be no end.*" (emphasis mine)

Gabriel's prophecy will be completely fulfilled when Messiah sets up His millennial kingdom in Zion (Jerusalem) on David's everlasting throne as the Jewish King of Israel. Messiah also prophesied about His millennial kingdom, as it is the day when He will sit on His throne of glory.

> Matthew 19:28, "So Jesus said to them, "Assuredly I say to you, that in the regeneration, when the Son of Man sits on the throne of His glory, you who have followed Me will also sit on twelve thrones, judging the twelve tribes of Israel."

When Jesus prophesied about the regeneration, He is speaking about the millennial reign when mankind and creation are "regenerated." We can also understand that Messiah is speaking of His Jewish kingdom at the millennial reign, as He states that the twelve Jewish disciples will sit on the twelve thrones, judging the twelve Jewish tribes of Israel (children of Israel-Jews). We see the exact same language in Revelation when the apostle John describes Messiah's millennial kingdom.

> Revelation 20:4, "*And I saw thrones, and they sat on them, and judgment was committed to them.* Then I saw the souls of those who had been beheaded for their witness to Jesus and for the word of God, who had not worshiped the beast or his image, and had not received his mark on their foreheads or on their hands. *And they lived and reigned with Christ for a thousand years.*" (emphasis mine)

The apostle John is prophesying about Jesus' thousand-year reign on earth, as Messiah will sit on His throne of glory. The book of Acts gives us great insight concerning Messiah's Jewish kingdom to come.

> Acts 1:6–7, "Therefore, when they had come together, they asked Him, saying, "Lord, will You at this time restore the kingdom to Israel?" And He said to them, "It is not for you to know times or seasons which the Father has put in His own authority."

The Jewish disciples asked the King of the Jews the time of His restoration of the kingdom of Israel and Judah (Jewish). Messiah confirmed the restoration of the Jewish kingdom as He did not rebuke or correct the disciples, but stated, "It is not for them to know the time or the seasons."

Make no mistake, the kingdom of Israel and Judah has always been and always will be Jewish! So, if you are saved by Jesus the Messiah, the Jewish kingdom is for you to proclaim, as well!

> Galatians 3:29, "And if you are Christ's, then you are Abraham's seed, and heirs according to the promise."

In the Gospels, Messiah confirmed that He is the King of the Jews.

Luke 23:3, "Then Pilate asked Him, saying, "Are You the King of the Jews?" He answered him and said, "It is as you say." (Matt. 27:11; Mark 15:2; John 18:33–37).

If Jesus is the King of the Jews and His heritage is Jewish (Joel 3:2), and He will reign from David's everlasting throne which is Jewish, then clearly His millennial and eternal kingdom will be Jewish. Let us not forget, Abraham, Isaac, Jacob, Joseph, the twelve tribes, Moses, the Old Testament saints, the major prophets, the twelve apostles, and Paul were all Jewish, as well. Luke also confirms the earthly Jewish kingdom during the millennial reign, including the fulfillment of the Abrahamic, Davidic, and New Covenants.

Acts 3:18–26, "But those things which God foretold by the mouth of all His prophets, that the Christ would suffer, He has thus fulfilled. Repent therefore and be converted, that your sins may be blotted out, so that times of refreshing may come from the presence of the Lord, and that He may send Jesus Christ, who was preached to you before, whom heaven must receive until the times of *restoration of all things*, which God has spoken by the mouth of all His holy prophets since the world began. For Moses truly said to the fathers, 'The Lord your God will raise up for you a Prophet like me from your brethren. Him you shall hear in all things, whatever He says to you. And it shall be that every soul who will not hear that Prophet shall be utterly destroyed from among the people.' Yes, and all the prophets, from Samuel and those who follow, as many as have spoken, have also foretold these days. You are sons of the prophets, and of the covenant which God made with our fathers, saying to Abraham, 'And in your seed all the families of the earth shall be blessed.' To you first, God, having raised up His Servant Jesus, sent Him to bless you, in turning away every one of you from your iniquities."

WHO WILL REIGN WITH MESSIAH?

Now, the question is, "Who will reign with Messiah during His millennial kingdom? The Old Testament saints? The tribulation saints? The raptured saints? The survivors of the great tribulation?"

The Old Testament saints will be resurrected to inherit God's promises of the everlasting covenants. It is imperative to understand that all of the promises of the covenants were made to Abraham, Isaac, Jacob, David, and their descendants, the Jewish people. Gentiles are "grafted into" these covenants (Rom. 11), and are included in the promises of the covenants (Gal. 3:29). The book of Hebrews and the prophet Daniel confirm that the Old Testament saints will be resurrected into their glorious bodies and receive the promised inheritance of the everlasting covenants from the Lord.

Hebrews 11:13–15, "These all died in faith, not having received the promises, but having seen them afar off were assured of them, embraced them and confessed that they were strangers and pilgrims on the earth. For those who say such things declare plainly that they seek a homeland. And truly if they had called to mind that country from which they had come out, they would have had opportunity to return" (Also see Heb. 11:8–10).

Daniel 12:1–2, "At that time Michael shall stand up, the great prince who stands watch over the sons of your people; And there shall be a time of trouble, such as never was since there was a nation, even to that time. And at that time your people (Jews) shall be delivered, every one who is found written in the book. And many of those who sleep in the dust of the earth shall awake, some to everlasting life, some to shame and everlasting contempt."

Daniel 12:13, "But you, go your way till the end; for you shall rest, and will arise to your inheritance at the end of the days."

The Old Testament saints, pre and post flood, including the Patriarchs and their faithful descendants, will reign with Messiah during His millennial kingdom. Now that we have verified that the Old Testament saints will reign with Messiah, John gives us understanding as to the tribulation and raptured saints.

Revelation 20:4–6, "And I saw thrones, and they sat on them, and judgment was committed to them. Then I saw the souls of those who had been beheaded for their witness to Jesus and for the word of God, who had not worshiped the beast or his image, and had not received his mark on their foreheads or on their hands. *And they lived and reigned with Christ for a thousand years.* But the rest of the dead (unbelievers) did not live again until the thousand years were finished. This is the first resurrection. Blessed and holy is he who has part in the first resurrection. Over such the second death has no power, *but they shall be priests of God and of Christ, and shall reign with Him a thousand years.*" (emphasis mine)

At the beginning of the prophecy, John is clearly speaking of the believers who are martyred (tribulation saints) during the Great Tribulation as, "they had not worshipped the Antichrist and received the mark of the beast." Clearly, the tribulation saints will reign with Messiah on earth for the thousand-year reign. As John continues, he tells us that the rest of the dead will not live again until the one-thousand years are finished. He is speaking of the dead that were not faithful to God before Messiah, and also the people who did not accept Jesus, as they are not included in the first resurrection. Please note, when a person died without being faithful to God before Messiah, and the people that die without accepting Jesus after His First Coming, they go to Hades (hell) until the Great White Throne Judgment. After Messiah's millennial reign on earth, the unbelievers will be delivered to the Great White Throne, and He will judge them according to their works written in the Book of Life (Rev. 20:11–15). After the Almighty's judgment, they will be cast into the lake of fire for eternity. John also states that he "saw thrones, and the people who sat on them, and judgment was committed to them." Who is he speaking of?

> Matthew 19:28, "So Jesus said to them, "Assuredly I say to you, that in the *regeneration*, when the Son of Man sits on the throne of His glory, you who have followed Me will also sit on twelve thrones, judging the twelve tribes of Israel." (emphasis mine)

Messiah confirms John's vision in Revelation 20:4–6. During the millennial reign, the disciples (apostles) will sit on the twelve thrones judging the twelve tribes of Israel. This substantiates that the disciples (apostles) will be resurrected, as well. So, if the saved disciples' in Jesus will be resurrected at this time, then all of the believers who are saved in Messiah will also be resurrected and reign with Him at His millennial kingdom! The first resurrection will include the Old Testament saints, the raptured saints, and the tribulation saints. These saints will serve as priests and kings of God and Messiah.

> Revelation 1:5–6, "To Him who loved us and washed us from our sins in His own blood, and has made us kings and priests to His God and Father, to Him be glory and dominion forever and ever." (Also see Rev. 3:21, 5:10)

2 Timothy 2:11–13, "This is a faithful saying: For if we died with Him, we shall also live with Him. *If we endure, we shall also reign with Him.* If we deny Him, He also will deny us. If we are faithless, He remains faithful; He cannot deny Himself."

The Old Testament saints, the raptured saints, and the tribulation saints will return with Messiah for His Second Coming and millennial reign!

Revelation 19:11–14, "Now I saw heaven opened, and behold, a white horse. And He who sat on him was called Faithful and True, and in righteousness He judges and makes war. His eyes were like a flame of fire, and on His head were many crowns. He had a name written that no one knew except Himself. He was clothed with a robe dipped in blood, and His name is called The Word of God. *And the armies in heaven, clothed in fine linen, white and clean, followed Him on white horses.*"

John confirms that all resurrected believers are following Messiah for His Second Coming. It is not logical that the saints would come down with Messiah and then return to heaven for a thousand years. There is not anywhere in the Holy Bible that suggests the saints return to heaven after coming with Messiah for His Second Coming. Furthermore, Messiah solidifies that the Old Testament saints, the raptured saints, and the tribulation saints will be resurrected and they will reign with Him during His millennial kingdom.

Luke 23:42–43, Then he said to Jesus, "Lord, remember me when You come into Your kingdom." And Jesus said to him, "Assuredly, I say to you, today you will be with Me in Paradise."

This is an imperative and profound statement for all believers to understand. Any time Jesus said *assuredly*, we can understand it as an emphatic promise and it will definitely happen! As the criminal was being crucified next to Messiah, he asked Messiah to remember him in His kingdom. Jesus replied, "Today, you will be with me in paradise." Messiah did not say once the kingdom was ready or after the great tribulation and millennial reign, He said today! As believers, we can rejoice and be comforted that when we pass away or if we are raptured, we will immediately be with the Lord in paradise, as well.

1 Thessalonians 4:17–18, "And thus we shall always be with the Lord. Therefore, comfort one another with these words."

Here are the groups of people that will reign with Messiah during the millennial kingdom in their glorified bodies (resurrected):

- Old Testament saints (before Messiah)
- Raptured (resurrected) saints (after Messiah)
- Tribulation saints (martyrs of Messiah during the tribulation period)

The believers who survive the tribulation, Jews and Gentiles, will live in their present physical body during the millennial reign. Zechariah prophesies about the remnant of the children of Israel that will live through the great tribulation unto the millennial reign.

Zechariah 13:8–9, "And it shall come to pass in all the land," says the Lord, "That two-thirds in it shall be cut off and die, *But one– third shall be left in it: I will bring the one–third through the fire, will refine them as silver is refined, and test them as gold is tested. They will call on My name, and I will answer them. I will say, 'This is My people'; And each one will say, 'The Lord is my God.'"* (Also see Rev. 7, 12:13–17)

During the millennial kingdom, although the survivors of the tribulation will have physical bodies, the saints (believers) will have glorified bodies that are immortal and incorruptible. We will not have to worry about cancer, diseases, broken bones, ailments, pain, suffering, or death!

> 1 Corinthians 15:53–57, "For this corruptible must put on incorruption, and this mortal must put on immortality. So when this corruptible has put on incorruption, and this mortal has put on immortality, then shall be brought to pass the saying that is written: "Death is swallowed up in victory." "O Death, where is your sting? O Hades, where is your victory?" The sting of death is sin, and the strength of sin is the law. But thanks be to God, who gives us the victory through our Lord Jesus Christ.

We can only imagine how beautiful and perfect our immortal bodies will be during Messiah's earthly kingdom. If our mortal bodies on Earth are made in the image and likeness of God (Gen. 1:26), our glorious immortal bodies will be even greater! Just as the saints (you and me) will receive new glorious bodies, God's creation will be cleansed and restored, as well.

At the end of the great tribulation period (Second Coming), God's creation will have endured the most horrific time in history (Rev. 6–19; Matt. 24:21). The Earth will have been damaged and polluted, buildings and cities ruined, roads and highways destroyed, basically an overall complete and total disaster (Isa. 24). However, after Messiah's Second Coming and during the millennial reign, God will restore His creation!

> Romans 8:18–23, "For I consider that the sufferings of this present time are not worthy to be compared with the glory which shall be revealed in us. *For the earnest expectation of the creation eagerly waits for the revealing of the sons of God.*

For the creation was subjected to futility, not willingly, but because of Him who subjected it in hope; because the creation itself also will be delivered from the bondage of corruption into the glorious liberty of the children of God. For we know that the whole creation groans and labors with birth pangs together until now. Not only that, but we also who have the firstfruits of the Spirit, even we ourselves groan within ourselves, eagerly waiting for the adoption, the redemption of our body." (emphasis mine)

Just as we eagerly await our immortal, incorruptible bodies, God's creation groans and labors with birth pangs for its glorious restoration, as well. Paul's prophecy describes how much God loves His creation, and how He will restore it back to its intended beauty and purpose. He states, "it will be delivered from the bondage of corruption and handed into the glorious liberty of the children of God," as the inhabitants of the world have disregarded its purpose and cast sin and pollution upon it. Paul prophesies that God's creation will be cleansed and restored, and given into the liberty of the saints during His thousand-year reign! In fact, the Promised Land (Israel) will be like the Garden of Eden and the cities and the ruins will be rebuilt, restored, and inhabited.

Ezekiel 36:33–38, "Thus says the Lord God: "On the day that I cleanse you from all your iniquities (Second Coming), I will also enable you to dwell in the cities, and the ruins shall be rebuilt. The desolate land shall be tilled instead of lying desolate in the sight of all who pass by. So they will say, '*This land that was desolate has become like the garden of Eden; and the wasted, desolate, and ruined cities are now fortified and inhabited.*' Then the nations which are left all around you shall know that I, the Lord, have rebuilt the ruined places and planted what was desolate. I, the Lord, have spoken it, and I will do it." Thus says the Lord God: "I will also let the house of Israel inquire of Me to do this for them: I will increase their men like a flock. Like a flock offered as holy sacrifices, like the flock at Jerusalem on its feast days, so shall the ruined cities be filled with flocks of men. Then they shall know that I am the Lord." (emphasis mine) (Also see Isa. 4:2–6, 51:3, 58:12; Ezek. 36:7– 15; Jer. 31:1–14; Zech. 13:1–6)

During Messiah's millennial kingdom, the Promised Land will be as the Garden of Eden! Ezekiel's prophecy should give our hearts great joy and excitement, because the original Garden of Eden was made in God's glory; Peace, love, happiness, order, and fulfillment, just to name a few. God made the Garden of Eden absolutely perfect for mankind's habitation (Gen. 2), so we can be confident that the environment was pure, clean, and naturally beautiful. During the millennial reign, the prophets declare that the cities and the ruins will be rebuilt, fortified, and inhabited. Since there will be mortal survivors from the great tribulation and Second Coming, children will be born during the millennial reign as God will "fill the cities with their flock."

Zechariah 9:16, "The Lord their God will save them in that day, as the flock of His people." (Also see Zech. 13:8–9)

All of these prophetic events will occur during the millennial reign in order to bring glory, honor, and praise to the King of Kings and Lord of Lords, the King of Israel, Jesus the Messiah. As the millennial reign begins, the restoration process will begin for mankind and creation, as well (regeneration). Messiah will comfort those who mourn and bless them with gifts for His glorification. The old ruins and cities will also be rebuilt during this time. The prophets Amos and Ezekiel not only confirm the rebuilding of the cities, but they also give us insight as to some of the occupations and activities that will occur during the millennial reign.

Amos 9:14–15, "Behold, the days are coming, says the Lord, "When the plowman shall overtake the reaper, and the treader of grapeshot who sows seed; The mountains shall drip with sweet wine, and all the hills shall flow with it." I will bring back the captives of My people Israel; They shall build the waste cities and inhabit them; They shall plant vineyards and drink wine from them; They shall also make gardens and eat fruit from them. I will plant them in their land, and no longer shall they be pulled up from the land I have given them," says the Lord your God."

Ezekiel 34:27, "Then the trees of the field shall yield their fruit, and the earth shall yield her increase. They shall be safe in their land; and they shall know that I am the Lord, when I have broken the bands of their yoke and delivered them from the hand of those who enslaved them." (Also see Ezek. 28:25–26)

The two prophets tell us there will be farming, gardening, vineyards, and that fruit trees will be planted. For all of us who love the outdoors, helping God plant His Garden of Eden will be an incredible experience. Amos and Ezekiel emphasize that at Messiah's millennial reign, He will plant the saints safely in the Promised Land, and no longer shall they be pulled up from there. The prophets are confirming the fulfillment of the everlasting covenants from God Almighty. As we verified, all of the saints are with Messiah in Jerusalem during the millennial reign (Also see 1 Thess. 4:16–17; Rev. 19:14).

It is imperative to understand that Messiah's millennial kingdom will have normal activities and occupations similar to what we experience today. The major difference will be the King of Israel, Jesus the Messiah, who will reign from Jerusalem on David's throne, establishing His government with righteous sovereignty (Isa. 9:6–

7)! Zechariah prophesied about the normal activities people will be doing during the millennial reign. For example, the elderly will be able to sit in the city streets as they once did, and children will be playing in the streets of Jerusalem.

> Zechariah 8:3–5, "Thus says the Lord: 'I will return to Zion, and dwell in the midst of Jerusalem. Jerusalem shall be called the City of Truth, the Mountain of the Lord of hosts, the Holy Mountain.' "Thus says the Lord of hosts: Old men and old women shall again sit in the streets of Jerusalem, each one with his staff in his hand because of great age. The streets of the city shall be full of boys and girls playing in its streets.'"

The millennial kingdom will also have government and order, construction and building, farming and gardening, and all of the other occupations we have today, including the rebuilding of roads and highways.

> Isaiah 35:8–10, "A highway shall be there, and a road, and it shall be called the Highway of Holiness. The unclean shall not pass over it, but it shall be for others. Whoever walks the road, although a fool, shall not go astray. No lion shall be there, nor shall any ravenous beast go up on it; It shall not be found there. But the redeemed shall walk there, and the ransomed of the Lord shall return, and come to Zion with singing, with everlasting joy on their heads. They shall obtain joy and gladness, and sorrow and sighing shall flee away."
> (Also see Isa. 49:11–13)

Isaiah is describing the peace, joy, and harmony that will fill Jerusalem and the Promised Land during the millennial reign. There will be a highway of holiness, where the resurrected saints will walk. The saints will return to Zion singing and praising the Lord with *everlasting joy. All of the resurrected saint's pain and sorrow will have vanished away. We can be confident that when Isaiah tells us that the lion and the beast will not be on the highway of holiness, that there will be animals, including the lion and the beast, living in other areas during the millennial reign.*

> Isaiah 33:20–22, "Look upon Zion, the city of our appointed feasts; Your eyes will see Jerusalem, a quiet home, a tabernacle that will not be taken down; Not one of its stakes will ever be removed, nor will any of its cords be broken. *But there the majestic Lord will be for us, a place of broad rivers and streams, in which no galley with oars will sail, nor majestic ships pass by* (For the Lord is our Judge, the Lord is our Lawgiver, the Lord is our King; He will save us)." (emphasis mine)

In Isaiah's prophecy, he refers to the millennial reign as "God's tabernacle," which includes David's everlasting throne that will never be taken down, removed, or it's cords broken. Jerusalem will have streams of rivers that will flow from its majestic glory.

Zechariah tells us that during the millennial kingdom we will have seasons, as well! He also certifies Isaiah's prophecy as two rivers of living waters will run from Jerusalem. One river will flow west to the Mediterranean Sea (western), and the other river will flow east to the Dead Sea (eastern).

> Zechariah 14:8–9, "And in that day it shall be that living waters shall flow from Jerusalem, half of them toward the eastern sea and half of them toward the western sea; In both summer and winter it shall occur. And the Lord shall be King over all the earth. In that day it shall be, "The Lord is one," and His name one."

Zechariah's prophecy will occur during the millennial reign, as the Lord shall be King over all of the earth. Also, one pure language will be restored to the saints. Mankind has not had one pure language since God confused the peoples' language at the Tower of Babel (Gen. 11:19). The pure language that Messiah spoke was Aramaic Hebrew, so we can be confident that it will be the language of the millennial kingdom, as well.

> Zephaniah 3:9, "For then I will restore to the peoples a pure language, that they all may call on the name of the Lord, to serve Him with one accord."

As we have discovered, Messiah's millennial reign will be very similar to the world we live in today. Again, the major difference will be that the King of Israel, Jesus, will rule the world. For believers, it will fulfill our prayers and wishes for the current age; righteousness, justice, and peace (shalom). This can only be achieved through the righteous sovereignty of Messiah, and will only be fulfilled during the millennial kingdom. The prophet Micah also gives us great wisdom and understanding of the millennial reign.

> Micah 4:1–3, "Now it shall come to pass in the latter days that the mountain of the Lord's house shall be established on the top of the mountains, and shall be exalted above the hills; And peoples shall flow to it. Many nations shall come and say, "Come, and let us go up to the mountain of the Lord, to the house of the God of Jacob; He will teach us His ways, and we shall walk in His paths." For out of Zion the law shall go forth, and the word of the Lord from Jerusalem. He shall judge between many peoples, and rebuke strong nations afar off; They shall beat their swords into plowshares, and their spears into pruning hooks; Nation shall not lift up sword against nation, neither shall they learn war anymore." (Also see Isa. 2:1–4).

Just as we discovered in the previous chapters, mountains are symbolic for kingdoms (Dan. 2:35). Micah is prophesying about the millennial reign as he states, "in the latter days, the mountain of the Lord's house shall be established on top of the mountains, and shall be exalted above the hills," meaning the Lord's kingdom (mountain) in Jerusalem shall be exalted above all other kingdoms (mountains) and nations (hills). Kings do not rule over mountains, but over kingdoms, thereby confirming that mountains are symbolic for kingdoms.

During the millennial reign, Micah states that many nations will come to the kingdom of the Lord (Jerusalem), and Messiah will teach the people His ways. As He continues, he clearly states that the Torah (law) and the Word of God will go out to all of the nations, as He judges and rebukes the nations that are far away (Mic. 4:2–3). Some Christians believe that the Torah is obsolete. This is a very dangerous point of view because Messiah emphatically stated that He will fulfill the Torah and the prophets (Matt. 5:17–18), confirming its importance and validity.

During the millennial reign, Micah also states that there will not be any war, as "nation shall not lift up a sword against nation, and they will turn their swords into plowshares and spears into pruning hooks." Can you imagine a world without the ongoing devastation and destruction of war and the evils that come with it? During Messiah's thousand-year reign, there will not be any more soldiers or civilians killed, wounded, or traumatized because of war! Hallelujah!

Isaiah prophesies that the surviving nations of the Second Coming events will come to Jerusalem and worship the King of Israel, Messiah. The nations will pay their respects and give honor to the King of Kings and Lord of Lords by bringing wealth, including gold, silver, incense, and animals to the City of the Lord (Zion), just as the wise men did when He was born (Matt. 2:11).

Isaiah 60:5–7, "Then you shall see and become radiant, and your heart shall swell with joy; Because the abundance of the sea shall be turned to you, the wealth of the Gentiles shall come to you. The multitude of camels shall cover your land, the dromedaries of Midian and Ephah; All those from Sheba shall come; They shall bring gold and incense, and they shall proclaim the praises of the Lord. All the flocks of Kedar shall be gathered together to you, the rams of Nebaioth shall minister to you; They shall ascend with acceptance on My altar, and I will glorify the house of My glory. Surely the coastlands shall wait for Me; And the ships of Tarshish will come first, to bring your sons from afar, their silver and their gold with them, to the name of the Lord your God, and to the Holy One of Israel, because He has glorified you." (Also see Isaiah 60:14–16).

During the millennial reign, all nations and people will come to Jerusalem to worship the King! Throughout history, evil kings and empires have tried to destroy Israel and forsake the children of Israel from God's everlasting promises. However, at Messiah's millennial reign, all people and all nations will understand that Jesus is the King, and His inheritance, His heritage, His land, and His people, Israel will be glorified and exalted! As Isaiah states, "He will make Israel an eternal excellence, a joy of many generations."

THE MILLENNIAL TEMPLE

During the millennial reign, the temple will be built in Jerusalem, as well! In the book of Ezekiel, chapters 40–48, Ezekiel gives us the blueprint of the Jewish temple, and He also tells us where Messiah will actually reside inside of it! As the Lord's angel guides Ezekiel through the vision, he explains in great detail the dimensions and arrangements of the temple. It is important to understand that Ezekiel is prophesying to the children of Israel who will be in their physical bodies (earthly bodies), not the glorified saints who have resurrected bodies (Ezek. 40:4, 43:10–11). All of the resurrected saints with their glorified bodies will be serving Messiah as priests and kings (Rev. 1:5–6, 2:26–27, 20:6).

Ezekiel 40:2–5, "In the visions of God He took me into the land of Israel and set me on a very high mountain; on it toward the south was something like the structure of a city. He took me there, and behold, there was a man whose appearance was like the appearance of bronze. He had a line of flax and a measuring rod in his hand, and he stood in the gateway. And the man said to me, "Son of man, look with your eyes and hear with your ears, and fix your mind on everything I show you; for you were brought here so that I might show them to you. Declare to the house of Israel everything you see." Now there was a wall all around the outside of the temple. In the man's hand was a measuring rod six cubits long, each being a cubit and a handbreadth; and he measured the width of the wall structure, one rod; and the height, one rod."

At the beginning of Ezekiel's vision in chapter 40, he is describing the Jewish Temple of the millennial kingdom because the New Jerusalem in "Eternity" does not have a temple (Rev. 21:22), as God Almighty and Messiah are its temple. In Ezekiel 40–42, he describes the dimensions of the floor plan, the eastern gateway of the temple, the outer court, the northern gateway, the southern gateway, the gateways of the inner court, the chambers, the inner court, the sanctuary, the temple area, and the outer dimensions of the temple, including the building at the Western end (Heb. 11:8–10). Ezekiel also explains that the city of Jerusalem will be located south of the temple (Ezek. 40:2). Please note, during the great tribulation and Second Coming, the topography of Jerusalem and the world will have changed (Rev. 6–19). As a result, Jerusalem will be divided into three parts by the great earthquake (Rev. 16:18–19). In Ezekiel 43, he describes the Lord's dwelling place, the dimensions of the altar, and also confirms that he is speaking of the temple during the millennial reign.

Ezekiel 43:6–9, "Then I heard Him speaking to me from the temple, while a man stood beside me. And He said to me,

"Son of man, this is the place of My throne and the place of the soles of My feet, where I will dwell in the midst of the children of Israel forever. No more shall the house of Israel defile My holy name, they nor their kings, by their harlotry or with the carcasses of their kings on their high places. When they set their threshold by My threshold, and their doorpost by My doorpost, with a wall between them and Me, they defiled My holy name by the abominations which they committed; therefore, I have consumed them in My anger. Now let them put their harlotry and the carcasses of their kings far away from Me, and I will dwell in their midst forever."

As we discussed, there is not a temple in the New Jerusalem (Rev. 21:22), so when Ezekiel states "I heard Him (Messiah) speaking from the temple," he is referring to the time of the millennial reign. Also, when Messiah states, "this is the place of My throne and the place of the soles of My feet," He confirms the prophecy of Zechariah (Zech. 14:4), where He will place His feet on the Mount of Olives at His Second Coming and set up His millennial kingdom. Furthermore, just as God's glory left Jerusalem and "stood" on the Mount of Olives at the east side of Jerusalem (Ezek. 11:23), His glory will return to Jerusalem and the temple from the east, as well!

Ezekiel 43:2, "And behold, the glory of the God of Israel came from the way of the east."

Ezekiel 43:4, "And the glory of the Lord came into the temple by way of the gate which faces toward the east."

Ezekiel is clearly referring to the millennial reign, because the glory of the Lord will come into the messianic temple. It is important to understand that only Messiah can enter and leave through the Eastern Gate, the Lion's Gate (Ezek. 44:1–2). In Ezekiel 45, he states that the Promised Land will be divided among the twelve tribes of

Israel as their inheritance, and he also confirms Messiah's inheritance of the land, as well.

> Ezekiel 45:1,4–5, "Moreover, when you divide the land by lot into inheritance, you shall set apart a district for the Lord, a holy section of the land; It shall be a holy section of the land, belonging to the priests, the ministers of the sanctuary, who come near to minister to the Lord; it shall be a place for their houses and a holy place for the sanctuary. An area twenty-five thousand cubits long and ten thousand wide shall belong to the Levites, the ministers of the temple; they shall have twenty chambers as a possession." (Ezek. 45:6–8)

The millennial kingdom's temple will have a district for the Lord (holy section) as well as holy places for the Levites (priests) in the sanctuary. In the book of Revelation, John gives us insight concerning the Levites during the millennial reign. At the time of the seven-year tribulation period, God will place a seal of protection on 144,000 of the twelve tribes of Israel (12,000 x 12, Rev. 7:3–8). The "sealed of Israel" will include 12,000 men of the priestly tribe of Levi (Deut. 18:1). The Levites will minister the gospel during the great tribulation, and they will continue to be ministers in their "physical state" during the millennial kingdom.

During the millennial reign, there will be a sacrificial system instituted at the temple of the Lord. It will be the only location in the world that will perform sacrifices of worship and celebration to the Lord.

Make no mistake, Messiah's crucifixion was the final atoning sacrifice for the world's sins, including yours and mine (Rom. 5:6–11); however, there will be burnt offerings and sacrifices during the millennial kingdom. A great example of this is our current communion service, as taking communion is a remembrance of what Messiah did on the cross for us. Likewise, during the millennial reign, the sacrifices and offerings will be a remembrance of what

Messiah did for the children of Israel in Egypt and after the Exodus, and also His crucifixion on the cross.

Zechariah 14:20–21, "In that day "HOLINESS TO THE LORD" shall be engraved on the bells of the horses. The pots in the Lord's house shall be like the bowls before the altar. Yes, every pot in Jerusalem and Judah shall be holiness to the Lord of hosts. *Everyone who sacrifices shall come and take them and cook in them.*" (emphasis mine)

The priestly Levites will make burnt offerings and sacrifices for the physical bodied people, reminding them of Messiah's transformation in their lives, just as communion does for us today. The resurrected saints will not need the offerings and sacrifices, as they will be in an eternal glorified state (1 Cor. 15:35–58). Only the high priests (Levites) will make the sacrifices and offerings for the people. Please note, although Satan is chained and bound during the millennial reign, the physical bodied people will still be sinful (Jer. 17:9–10). Until they receive their resurrected bodies, they will not be incorruptible and immortal. The apostle Paul gives us great wisdom and understanding of the sacrificial system during the millennial reign.

Hebrews 10:1–10, "For the law, having a shadow of the good things to come, and not the very image of the things, can never with these same sacrifices, which they offer continually year by year, make those who approach perfect. For then would they not have ceased to be offered? For the worshipers, once purified, would have had no more consciousness of sins. But in those sacrifices there is a reminder of sins every year. For it is not possible that the blood of bulls and goats could take away sins. Therefore, when He came into the world, He said: "Sacrifice and offering You did not desire, but a body You have prepared for Me. In burnt offerings and sacrifices for sin

You had no pleasure. Then I said, 'Behold, I have come, in the volume of the book it is written of Me—To do Your will, O God.'" Previously saying, "Sacrifice and offering, burnt offerings, and offerings for sin You did not desire, nor had pleasure in them" (which are offered according to the law), then He said, "Behold, I have come to do Your will, O God." He takes away the first that He may establish the second. By that will we have been sanctified through the offering of the body of Jesus Christ once for all."

The children of Israel never fulfilled the Torah (Mosaic Covenant) because they continually rebelled and sinned against God. This is one of the reasons why Messiah stated He will fulfill the Torah and the prophets (Matt. 5:17–18), as the children of Israel never fulfilled their duty of its righteous purpose.

Isaiah 46:10, "Declaring the end from the beginning, and from ancient times things that are not yet done, saying, 'My counsel shall stand, and I will do all My pleasure.'"

Again, the sacrificial system during the millennial reign does not diminish Messiah's atonement for our sins on the cross in any way, but it will actually fulfill the Old Testament practice (Torah) that He commanded.

Ezekiel 44:11, 14, "Yet they shall be ministers in My sanctuary, as gatekeepers of the house and ministers of the house; they shall slay the burnt offering and the sacrifice for the people, and they shall stand before them to minister to them. I will make them keep charge of the temple, for all its work, and for all that has to be done in it."

Ezekiel confirms that the Torah will be fulfilled, including sacrifices and offerings. Also, God states that the Levites shall be ministers in "My sanctuary," referring to the Jewish Temple during the millennial kingdom. There will also be grain and peace offerings, as well.

> Ezekiel 45:15–16, "And one lamb shall be given from a flock of two hundred, from the rich pastures of Israel. These shall be for grain offerings, burnt offerings, and peace offerings, to make atonement for them," says the Lord God. "All the people of the land shall give this offering for the prince in Israel."

Ezekiel is prophesying about the millennial kingdom, as the physical bodied people of the land will come before the Prince of Israel and give offerings. As we discussed, there will be a river flowing from the temple in Jerusalem to the Dead Sea (Ezek. 47:1–6). This prophecy also confirms that Ezekiel is not referring to the New Jerusalem (Eternity), because there will not be a "Sea" there (Rev. 21:1).

> Ezekiel 47:8–10, 12, Then he said to me: "This water flows toward the eastern region, goes down into the valley, and enters the sea. When it reaches the sea, its waters are healed. And it shall be that every living thing that moves, wherever the rivers go, will live. There will be a very great multitude of fish, because these waters go there; for they will be healed, and everything will live wherever the river goes. It shall be that fishermen will stand by it from En Gedi to En Eglaim; they will be places for spreading their nets. Their fish will be of the same kinds as the fish of the Great Sea, exceedingly many. Along the bank of the river, on this side and that, will grow all kinds of trees used for food; their leaves will not wither, and their fruit will not fail. They will bear fruit every month, because their water flows from the sanctuary. Their fruit will be for food, and their leaves for medicine."

In this extraordinary prophecy, the water will run from the temple into the Dead Sea (eastern), and it will heal the sea and every living creature in it, wherever the river runs. The salty Dead Sea will be transformed into a freshwater living sea! For all of the people who love to fish, it will be fishermen's paradise because there will be an abundance of fish to catch!

Ezekiel also describes a beautiful scene of fruit trees along the banks of the river that flows to the Dead Sea. The fruit will be used for food as well as medicine. This is a prophetic foreshadow of the Tree of Life (Rev. 22:2) in Eternity. The Lord prophesied that the Promised Land would be like the Garden of Eden, and this is a spectacular glimpse of His righteous sovereignty!

> Psalm 46:4, "There is a river whose streams shall make glad the city of God, the holy place of the tabernacle of the Most High."

In Ezekiel 47, Ezekiel explains how the Promised Land will be divided among the twelve tribes of Israel during the millennial kingdom.

> Ezekiel 47:13–14, 21, "Thus says the Lord God: "These are the borders by which you shall divide the land as an inheritance among the twelve tribes of Israel. Joseph shall have two portions. You shall inherit it equally with one another; for I raised My hand in an oath to give it to your fathers, and this land shall fall to you as your inheritance. Thus you shall divide this land among yourselves according to the tribes of Israel. It shall be that you will divide it by lot as an inheritance for yourselves."

The twelve tribes of Israel will receive their promised inheritance at the beginning of the millennial reign. In Ezekiel 48:1–7, seven of the twelve tribes will be north of Messiah's inheritance (Ezek. 45:1), the holy district: Judah, Reuben, Ephraim, Manasseh, Naphtali,

Asher, and Dan. Ephraim and Manasseh were Joseph's sons, accounting for the double inheritance (Ezek. 47:13). Judah, the tribe of Messiah (Rev. 5:5), will be the closest tribe in proximity to Him (holy district) on the northern side of the temple.

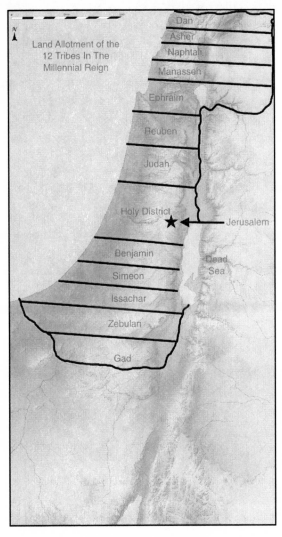

Millennial Land Allotment

In Ezekiel 48:23–29, the remaining five tribes will be located south of the holy district. The closest tribe in proximity to the holy district will be Benjamin, who is Joseph's pure younger brother from Rachel, who only gave birth to the two of them. Then, continuing southward in order of their geographical locations are Simeon, Issachar, Zebulun, and Gad. In Ezekiel 48:30–34, the dimensions of the city are given, and Ezekiel tells us there will be three gates on each side (twelve gates). Each gate will be named after one of the twelve tribes of Israel based on the birthmother of the tribe. The closest tribes to the holy district were birthed by or through Rachel. The outer tribes were birthed by maidservants. The tribes inhabiting the holy portion and north were born by Leah, Jacob's (Israel's) first wife. Ezekiel also tells us the name of the city.

Ezekiel 48:35, "The name of the city from that day shall be, "THE LORD IS THERE."

TRIBE -IN ORDER OF LAND ALLOTMENT	BIRTH MOTHER	GATE OF THE CITY
Dan	Bilhah (Rachel's maid)	East Gate
Asher	Zilpah (Leah's maid)	West Gate
Naphtali	Bilhah (Rachel's maid)	West Gate
Manasseh/Ephraim	Rachel (through Joseph)	East gate (named Joseph)
Reuben	Leah	North Gate
Judah	Leah	North gate
Levi (Zadok)	Leah	North gate
Benjamin	Rachel	East gate
Simeon	Leah	South gate
Issachar	Leah	South gate
Zebulun	Leah	South gate
Gad	Zilpah (Leah's maid)	West gate

Millennial Land Allotment

King Solomon, in his great wisdom, wrote a beautiful Psalm about the endless reign of Messiah, the perfect King.

PSALM 72

"Give the king Your judgments, O God, and Your righteousness to the king's Son. He will judge Your people with righteousness, and Your poor with justice. The mountains will bring peace to the people, and the little hills, by righteousness. He will bring justice to the poor of the people; He will save the children of the needy, and will break in pieces the oppressor. They shall fear You as long as the sun and moon endure, throughout all generations. He shall come down like rain upon the grass before mowing, like showers that water the earth. In His days the righteous shall flourish, and abundance of peace, until the moon is no more. He shall have dominion also from sea to sea, and from the River to the ends of the earth. Those who dwell in the wilderness will bow before Him, and His enemies will lick the dust. The kings of Tarshish and of the isles will bring presents; The kings of Sheba and Seba will offer gifts. Yes, all kings shall fall down before Him; All nations shall serve Him. For He will deliver the needy when he cries, the poor also, and him who has no helper. He will spare the poor and needy, and will save the souls of the needy. He will redeem their life from oppression and violence; and precious shall be their blood in His sight. And He shall live; And the gold of Sheba will be given to Him; Prayer also will be made for Him continually, and daily He shall be praised. There will be an abundance of grain in the earth, on the top of the mountains; Its fruit shall wave like Lebanon; And those of the city shall flourish like grass of the earth. His name shall endure forever; His name shall continue as long as the sun. And men shall be blessed in Him; All nations shall call Him blessed. Blessed be the Lord God, the God of Israel, Who only does wondrous things! And blessed be His glorious name forever! And let the whole earth be filled with His glory. Amen and Amen."

After the millennial reign ends, Messiah's everlasting kingdom will continue forever and ever! However, before Messiah makes everything new, including a new heaven and a new earth, the serpent of old, Satan, will be released for a short time (Rev. 20:3). Why is

Satan not cast into the lake of fire with the Antichrist and the false prophet at Messiah's Second Coming? Why is he released after the millennial reign for a short time?

One reason is to allow the people who were born during the millennial reign to be tempted and tested by Satan, as Messiah gives all people free will to accept or deny Him. Just as we have free will to choose our eternal destiny, heaven or hell, the physical bodied people that lives during the millennial kingdom will also have a choice. In order for that to happen, Satan will be released one final time. John confirms that Satan is released after the one-thousand years, as he gathers all of the mortal millennial unbelievers for one final battle.

Revelation 20:7–8, "Now when the thousand years have expired, Satan will be released from his prison and will go out to deceive the nations which are in the four corners of the earth, Gog and Magog, to gather them together to battle, whose number is as the sand of the sea."

Satan gathers the mortal unbelievers who are numbered "as the sand of the sea" (Rev. 20:8). Although Messiah reigns for one-thousand years from Jerusalem on David's everlasting throne, this clearly proves that there will be people who will choose not to follow and be saved by Him. Although Satan is "chained and bound" during the millennial reign, mankind's hearts (physical bodies) are still sinful. Many people will benefit and enjoy the Lord's blessings during this time without believing in Him.

John 2:24–25, "But Jesus did not commit Himself to them, because He knew all men, and had no need that anyone should testify of man, for He knew what was in man."

Another reason why Satan will be released at the end of the one thousand years is because Messiah has to fulfill all of the prophecies in the Holy Bible. According to God's prophetic timeline, Messiah will bring all things in the current heaven and earth under Him to give to God the Father. This will only occur when Messiah establishes His earthly millennial reign as King and destroys all enemies, dominions, principalities, authorities, and powers opposed to Him, delivering the kingdom to God the Father!

1 Corinthians 15:22–28, "For as in Adam all die, even so in Christ all shall be made alive. But each one in his own order: Christ the firstfruits, afterward those who are Christ's at His coming. *Then comes the end, when He delivers the kingdom to God the Father, when He puts an end to all rule and all authority and power. For He must reign till He has put all enemies under His feet. The last enemy that will be destroyed is death. For "He has put all things under His feet." But when He says "all things are put under Him," it is evident that He who put all things under Him is excepted.* Now when all things are made subject to Him, then the Son Himself will also be subject to Him who put all things under Him, *that God may be all in all."* (emphasis mine)

After the one-thousand years expire, Satan is allowed to deceive the nations one final time. Gog and Magog are the names of the evil nations that will join Satan and battle against the Lord in Jerusalem. Unlike Armageddon, where Satan battles the saints until the Lord returns for His Second Coming, this final battle will not be a contest whatsoever! God will send fire from heaven to consume and destroy Satan and his armies (Rev. 20:9). All of the evil people and nations will be destroyed at this time. Then, Satan will be cast into the lake of fire and brimstone and will be tormented with the Antichrist and the false prophet forever and ever! Hallelujah!

Revelation 20:9–10, "They went up on the breadth of the earth and surrounded the camp of the saints and the beloved city. And fire came down from God out of heaven and devoured them. The devil, who deceived them, was cast into the lake of fire and brimstone where the beast and the false prophet are. And they will be tormented day and night forever and ever."(Also see Isa. 14:15, 19)

After the victory is won by Messiah, the second resurrection and the Great White Throne Judgment will occur.

Revelation 20:11–12, "Then I saw a great white throne and Him who sat on it, from whose face the earth and the heaven fled away. And there was found no place for them. And I saw the dead, small and great, standing before God, and books were opened."

The Great White Throne Judgment is also known as the second death. It is Messiah's final judgment of two different groups of the dead. The first group includes all of the people who did not trust in God and obey His commandments before Messiah. The second group of the dead are the people who did not accept Jesus as their Messiah after His First Coming. All of the dead throughout history, including those who are in hades, will be judged according to their works. This is a very important point for us to understand because it deals with the dead only. John does not mention anyone else but the dead. If a person has been resurrected by the Lord (Old Testament saints, raptured saints, tribulation saints, millennial saints), the second death of the Great White Throne Judgment has no power over them (Rev. 20:6). The millennial saints (physical-bodied believers who lived during the thousand years) will have been resurrected and given immortal bodies at some point during this time as well, so the Great White Throne Judgment does not apply to them either. The Holy Bible does not specifically state when the millennial saints will receive their glorious body, but Paul confirms it will happen (1 Cor. 15:53–55). The permanent separation between the righteous and the wicked will occur at the Great White Throne Judgment.

Revelation 20:15, "And anyone not found written in the Book of Life was cast into the lake of fire."

Remember, the glorified saints (Old Testament saints, raptured saints, and tribulation saints) will be with Messiah during the millennial reign, serving as kings and priests. It is not logical that they would have to be judged again at this event. The glorified saints will have already appeared before the judgment seat of Messiah and received their rewards (2 Cor. 5:10) before the Second Coming. Just as John declares, if a person is a part of the first resurrection, then the second death has no power over them.

Revelation 20:5, 6, "But the rest of the dead did not live again until the thousand years were finished. This is the first resurrection. Blessed and holy is he who has part in the first resurrection. Over such the second death has no power, but they shall be priests of God and of Christ, and shall reign with Him a thousand years. (Also see Rev. 2:11, 2:26)

Revelation 20:12–15, "And another book was opened, which is the Book of Life. And the dead were judged according to their works, by the things which were written in the books. The sea gave up the dead who were in it, and Death and Hades delivered up the dead who were in them. And they were judged, each one according to his works. Then Death and Hades were cast into the lake of fire. This is the second death. And anyone not found written in the Book of Life was cast into the lake of fire."

The dead (unbelievers) will be judged according to their works that are written in the books, and anyone not found in the Book of Life will be cast into the lake of fire. As Satan, the Antichrist, and the False Prophet will be cast into the lake of fire, Death and Hades will also be cast into it, as well! Thus, Satan, the Antichrist, the False Prophet, and all nonbelievers will be tormented in the lake of fire forever and ever.

Matthew 6:9–10, "In this manner, therefore, pray: Our Father in heaven, hallowed be Your name. *Your kingdom come. Your will be done on earth as it is in heaven.*" (emphasis mine)

CHAPTER 11

THE NEW JERUSALEM

Revelation 21:3, 22:5, "And I heard a loud voice from heaven saying, "Behold, the tabernacle of God is with men, and He will dwell with them, and they shall be His people. God Himself will be with them and be their God. And they shall reign forever and ever.""

After the Millennial Reign and the Great White Throne Judgment, the New Jerusalem is introduced to the saints. At that point on God's prophetic timeline, all of God's saints, the Old Testament saints, the raptured saints, the tribulation saints, and the millennial saints, will inherit a new heaven and a new earth, and reign with Him forever and ever!

Revelation 21:1, "Now I saw a new heaven and a new earth, for the first heaven and the first earth had passed away."

According to the Word of God, the existing heaven and earth will not last forever in its current state. God Almighty will shake heaven and earth one last time to remove all things that are made from things that cannot be shaken. Only His eternal kingdom, the New Jerusalem will remain, as He will shake and remove the current heaven and earth, including the planets, sun, moon, stars, and other heavenly bodies.

Hebrews 12:26–28, "But now He has promised, saying, "Yet once more I shake not only the earth, but also heaven." Now this, "Yet once more," indicates the removal of those things that are being shaken, as of things that are made, that the things which cannot be shaken may remain."

When Messiah shakes the heavens and the earth, He will have fulfilled all of the Torah and the prophets (Matthew 5:17–18), which includes the everlasting covenants. He will then deliver the kingdom to the Father, God Almighty (Yahweh), so that He may be all in all!

1 Corinthians 15:24–28, "Then comes the end, when He delivers the kingdom to God the Father, when He puts an end to all rule and all authority and power. For He must reign till He has put all enemies under His feet. The last enemy that will be destroyed is death. For "He has put all things under His feet." But when He says "all things are put under Him," it is evident that He who put all things under Him is excepted. Now when all things are made subject to Him, then the Son Himself will also be subject to Him who put all things under Him, *that God may be all in all.*" (Also see Eph. 1:7–12) (emphasis mine)

When Messiah delivers the kingdom to the Father, all of His enemies will be under His feet, and all other rule, authority, power, including death will be destroyed forever. Isaiah gives us great insight about the new heavens and new earth once Messiah "puts all things under His feet."

Isaiah 65:17–19, "For behold, I create new heavens and a new earth; And the former shall not be remembered or come to mind. But be glad and rejoice forever in what I create; For behold, I create Jerusalem as a rejoicing, and her people a joy. I will rejoice in Jerusalem, and joy in My people."

Isaiah explains that the Almighty will create new heavens and a new earth, as the former heaven and earth will not be remembered. This will be an incredible feeling for the saints, because all of the evil of this world, such as idolatry, murder, disease, injustices, addictions, pain, suffering, etc., will no longer exist!

God commands us to rejoice in His spectacular creation, the New Jerusalem, just as He will rejoice with His saints in the eternal city. The New Jerusalem will be a place of total peace, love, comfort, and grace, and we should always have an eternal mindset that is clearly focused on God's glorious eternal kingdom, where His righteousness dwells (2 Peter 3:13).

Isaiah also prophesies about the dramatic contrast between the saints and the unbelievers in Eternity. The saints will be living in eternal harmony in the New Jerusalem (heaven), while the unbelievers will be tormented alive night and day in the eternal lake of fire.

Isaiah 66:22–24, "For as the new heavens and the new earth which I will make shall remain before Me," says the Lord, "So shall your descendants and your name remain. And it shall come to pass that from one New Moon to another, and from one Sabbath to another, all flesh shall come to worship before Me," says the Lord. *"And they shall go forth and look upon the corpses of the men who have transgressed against Me. For their worm does not die, and their fire is not quenched. They shall be an abhorrence to all flesh."* (2 Peter 3:5–9)

In this sobering prophecy, Isaiah explains that the saints in the eternal kingdom will worship the Lord and will be able to look upon the unbeliever's corpses who have been cast into the lake of fire. They will be tormented throughout eternity. Isaiah states, "for their worm does not die, and their fire is not quenched," thereby confirming that the unbelievers will be "alive" during their eternal torment (Revelation 14:9–11). I believe it is safe to say that all of mankind should desire to be on God's side! As John continues, he describes the holy city, the New Jerusalem.

> Revelation 21:2–3, "Then I, John, saw the holy city, New Jerusalem, coming down out of heaven from God, prepared as a bride adorned for her husband. And I heard a loud voice from heaven saying, "Behold, the *tabernacle* of God is with men, and He will dwell with them, and they shall be His people. God Himself will be with them and be their God."

The New Jerusalem will descend from God on the Feast of Tabernacles, and God Himself "will tabernacle and dwell among the saints." He will be our God, and we will be His people. John describes the beauty of the New Jerusalem, as "a bride adorned for her husband." Those who are married can relate to the euphoric moment of becoming one with their soul mate. For now, we can only dream and picture the glorious scene that we will experience in the New Jerusalem with God Almighty and Messiah, for forever and ever! Without question, the ultimate perfect marriage covenant is between Messiah and mankind.

> Revelation 19:6–7, 9, "Alleluia! For the Lord God Omnipotent reigns! Let us be glad and rejoice and give Him glory, *for the marriage of the Lamb has come, and His wife has made herself ready. Blessed are those who are called to the marriage supper of the Lamb!*" (emphasis mine)

In the book of John, John uses similar terminology about the "marriage supper of the Lamb," as he did in Revelation. He records that John the Baptist, Messiah's foreshadow, speaks of Him as the bridegroom searching for His bride, who are the saints (you and me).

> John 3:27, 29, 33–36, "John answered and said, "He who has the bride is the bridegroom; but the friend of the

bridegroom, who stands and hears him, rejoices greatly because of the bridegroom's voice. He who has received His testimony has certified that God is true. For He whom God has sent speaks the words of God, for God does not give the Spirit by measure. The Father loves the Son, and has given all things into His hand. He who believes in the Son has everlasting life; and he who does not believe the Son shall not see life, but the wrath of God abides on him."

Messiah is the one and only everlasting bridegroom searching for His bride. He is above all, the name higher than every other name (Phil. 2:9; Eph. 1:21). The people who accept Jesus as their Messiah will inherit everlasting life, and reign with Him in the New Jerusalem for eternity. It does not matter the color of your skin, your gender, what part of the world you live in, or anything else. If you accept Jesus as your Messiah, you will be saved (Romans 10:13; Acts 2:21). The apostle Paul speaks of the mystery of Messiah and His bride.

Ephesians 5:29–32, "For no one ever hated his own flesh, but nourishes and cherishes it, just as the Lord does the church. For we are members of His body, of His flesh and of His bones. "For this reason a man shall leave his father and mother and be joined to his wife, and the two shall become one flesh." *This is a great mystery, but I speak concerning Christ and the church.*" (emphasis mine)

Paul explains that we will become "one" with Messiah, just as a husband and wife become one in marriage. During Messiah's ministry on Earth, and before His crucifixion, He prayed to God the Father for all of the believers to become "one" with Him (John 17:20–26).

In the New Jerusalem, the division among the people including the church (denominations) will no longer exist. All of the saints will live together in unity with God and Messiah throughout eternity. What a great day it will be when all of the saints live together as one and experience the infinite, supreme, and everlasting glory of the Almighty! Hallelujah!

> Ephesians 2:19–22, "Now, therefore, you are no longer strangers and foreigners, but fellow citizens with the saints and members of the household of God, having been built on the foundation of the apostles and prophets, Jesus Christ Himself being the chief cornerstone, in whom the whole building, being fitted together, grows into a holy temple in the Lord, in whom you also are being built together for a dwelling place of God in the Spirit."

Regardless of how hard we strive to live a peaceful, fruitful, and joyful life on this earth, it is impossible for us to do so, as we are sinners. However, in the New Jerusalem, God Himself will bring ultimate peace, comfort, love, joy, and happiness!

> Revelation 21:4, "And God will wipe away every tear from their eyes; there shall be no more death, nor sorrow, nor crying. There shall be no more pain, for the former things have passed away."

Isaiah also prophesies about God destroying the last enemy, which is death. At that time, the saints will rejoice in the comfort of His salvation in the New Jerusalem.

> Isaiah 25:8, "He will swallow up death forever, and the Lord God will wipe away tears from all faces."

Certainly, Messiah is the Alpha and the Omega, the Beginning and the End, the First and the Last, the King of Kings, the Lord of Lords, the Almighty!

Revelation 21:6, "And He said to me, "It is done! I am the Alpha and the Omega, the Beginning and the End. I will give of the fountain of the water of life freely to him who thirsts."

Messiah gives eternal life freely to all people who believe in Him. Just as God finished the work of creation (Genesis 2:1–3), and Messiah finished the work of redemption and salvation (John 19:30), the Holy Trinity (Father, Son, and Holy Spirit) will finish God's prophetic timeline.

When Messiah cries, "It is done," we can understand it to be finalized. There is not anything or anyone, including Satan, that can reverse His will! John gives us some examples of this phrase in the Holy Bible:

1. The first time is when Messiah was praying in the Garden of Gethsemane before His crucifixion. (John 17:1–5)
2. The second time is when Messiah hung on the cross and was about to die for all of mankind's sins. (John 19:28–30)
3. The third time is in Revelation. Just as the seventh angel poured out the final judgment (seventh bowl) on the Earth, Messiah stated, "It is finished!" (Rev. 16:17–18)

In the New Jerusalem, when Messiah says, "It is finished," He is declaring the completion of His work, the restoration of creation and mankind to Him and the Father, as He is the author and the finisher of creation and mankind!

Hebrews 12:2, "Looking unto Jesus, the author and finisher of our faith, who for the joy that was set before Him endured the cross, despising the shame, and has sat down at the right hand of the throne of God."

THE NEW JERUSALEM

John 14:1–4, "Let not your heart be troubled; you believe in God, believe also in Me. In My Father's house are many mansions; if it were not so, I would have told you. I go to prepare a place for you. And if I go and prepare a place for you, I will come again and receive you to Myself; that where I am, there you may be also. And where I go you know, and the way you know."

In one of the most comforting and exciting verses in the Holy Bible, Messiah promises His saints the inheritance of the New Jerusalem! He tells us not to worry about the present life, because He has prepared heavenly mansions for you and me! We can only imagine how beautiful and majestic the New Jerusalem will be.

1 Corinthians 2:9, "But as it is written: "Eye has not seen, nor ear heard, nor have entered into the heart of man the things which God has prepared for those who love Him.""

If the Creator of the universe has blessed us with the incredibly gorgeous world we live in today, how much more beautiful will the New Jerusalem be that Messiah is preparing for us! John describes a glimpse of its beauty to us.

Revelation 21:10–13, "And he carried me away in the Spirit to a great and high mountain, and showed me the great city, the holy Jerusalem, descending out of heaven from God, having the glory of God. Her light was like a most precious stone, like a jasper stone, clear as crystal. Also she had a great and high wall with twelve gates, and twelve angels at the gates, and names written on them, which are the names of the twelve tribes of the children of Israel: three gates on the east, three gates on the north, three gates on the south, and three gates on the west."

John describes the New Jerusalem as descending out of heaven from the glory of God. In Psalm 19:1, King David states, "the heavens declare the glory of God." We have all witnessed beautiful sunrises and sunsets rising up in the horizon beyond the ocean or over the mountain tops, declaring God's glory in the heavens. Also at night, when the heavens are brightened from the brilliance of the stars. We can only imagine how much greater the glory of the New Jerusalem will be as it descends from God, basking in all of His glory!

John continues to give us details of the New Jerusalem when he describes it, "like a precious clear jasper stone." He also explains that the New Jerusalem will have a great wall with twelve angels at the twelve gates. There will be three gates on the north, south, east, and west, and each gate will have the name of one tribe of the twelve tribes of Israel. Isaiah also prophesied about the walls and gates of the New Jerusalem, as both will be adorned with colorful gems, sapphires, rubies, and crystal.

> Isaiah 54:11–13, "Behold, I will lay your stones with colorful gems, and lay your foundations with sapphires. I will make your pinnacles of rubies, Your gates of crystal, and all your walls of precious stones. All your children shall be taught by the Lord, and great shall be the peace of your children."

Isaiah also gives us great comfort in that the Lord will teach us His ways and we will have total shalom! As John continues his prophecy concerning the New Jerusalem, he describes the dimensions of the city.

> Revelation 21:14–17, "Now the wall of the city had twelve foundations, and on them were the names of the twelve apostles of the Lamb. And he who talked with me had a gold reed to measure the city, its gates, and its wall. The city is laid out as a square; its length is as great as its breadth. And he measured the city with the reed: twelve thousand furlongs. Its length, breadth, and height are equal. Then he measured

its wall: one hundred and forty-four cubits, according to the measure of a man, that is, of an angel."

Just as the twelve gates to the city will have the names of the twelve tribes of Israel written on them (Revelation 21:12–13), the twelve foundations will have the names of Messiah's twelve apostles written on them. Symbolically, the twelve tribes of Israel could represent the faithful saints in the Old Testament, and the twelve apostles could represent the faithful saints of the "church." Both will live together as one in the New Jerusalem. The city's measurements give us tremendous knowledge into God's infinite wisdom. The measurements are all multiples of twelve, which is the number associated with God's people:

- 12 Tribes of Israel
- 12 Apostles
- 12 layers to the walls, which are 144 cubits (12 x 12)
- 12 gates to the city, the height, length, and breadth are all the same, which is 12,000 furlongs, which is 1,400 miles squared, which is a perfect cube.

We can understand the New Jerusalem as being foursquare, which means it is a cube. The New Jerusalem will be 1,400 miles in length, 1,400 miles in height, and 1,400 miles in breadth. To give us an idea of the New Jerusalem, the length of the holy city (1,400 miles) is similar to the distance between Miami to Chicago or Dallas to Washington, DC. We can only imagine the magnitude of greatness of the New Jerusalem for 1,400 miles in height, in length, and in breadth! Also, the city walls are 144 cubits, which is 216 feet thick. John continues to give us a beautiful description of the foundation, the walls, and the city.

Revelation 21:18–21, "The construction of its wall was of jasper; and the city was pure gold, like clear glass. The foundations of the wall of the city were adorned with all kinds of precious stones: the first foundation was jasper, the second sapphire, the third chalcedony, the fourth emerald, the fifth sardonyx, the sixth sardius, the seventh chrysolite, the eighth beryl, the ninth topaz, the tenth chrysoprase, the eleventh jacinth, and the twelfth amethyst. The twelve gates were twelve pearls: each individual gate was of one pearl. And the street of the city was pure gold, like transparent glass."

John's illustration explains that the New Jerusalem is made of pure gold, and will be adorned with gorgeous precious stones. The construction of its wall is of jasper. The twelve foundations of the wall of the New Jerusalem will consist of the listed precious stones in the order of the foundations. The gorgeous description of the walls embedded with jewels reveals the purity, strength, and elegance of the New Jerusalem!

Additionally, all twelve gates are pearls, as each individual gate is a majestic pearl! Can you imagine the size of the pearly gates? Without question, it will be an eternal paradise adorned for the King and His saints.

THE GLORY OF THE NEW JERUSALEM

Revelation 21:22–23, "But I saw no temple in it, for the Lord God Almighty and the Lamb *are* its temple. The city had no need of the sun or of the moon to shine in it, for the glory of God illuminated it. *The Lamb is its light.*"

God, Messiah, and the Holy Spirit (Holy Trinity) are omnipotent, omniscient, and omnipresent, and His glory will illuminate the New Jerusalem. There will not be any need for a temple, sun, moon, or anything else, as the Lamb (Messiah) is its light!

Isaiah 60:19–20, "The sun shall no longer be your light by day, nor for brightness shall the moon give light to you; But the Lord will be to you an everlasting light, and your God your glory. Your sun shall no longer go down, nor shall your moon withdraw itself; For the Lord will be your everlasting light, and the days of your mourning shall be ended."

John 8:12, "Then Jesus spoke to them again, saying, "I am the light of the world. He who follows Me shall not walk in darkness, but have the light of life.""

John continues:

Revelation 21:24–27, "And the nations of those who are saved shall walk in its light, and the kings of the earth bring their glory and honor into it. Its gates shall not be shut at all by day (there shall be no night there). And they shall bring the glory and the honor of the nations into it. But there shall by no means enter it anything that defiles, or causes an abomination or a lie, but only those who are written in the Lamb's Book of Life."

When John writes, "And the nations of those who are saved shall walk in its light, and the kings of the earth shall bring their glory and honor into it," he is referring to the saved saints of the nations. Only the saints who are saved will be allowed to walk in His light, the New Jerusalem. Remember, the saints (you and me) will become kings and priests during the millennial reign (Rev. 5:9–10).

Clearly, only the saints (kings and priests) who are written in the Book of Life will inhabit the glorious New Jerusalem. Also, the beautiful pearly gates will never be closed, confirming that all evil has been destroyed and removed. The saints will dwell safe in the New Jerusalem with God and Messiah forever and ever! There will only be day (light) in the New Jerusalem, as night will no longer exist.

Just as God separated the light from the darkness in the beginning (Gen. 1:3–4), He will also divide it again in the New Jerusalem.

THE RIVER OF LIFE

Revelation 22:1–5, "And he showed me a pure river of water of life, clear as crystal, proceeding from the throne of God and of the Lamb. In the middle of its street, and on either side of the river, was the tree of life, which bore twelve fruits, each tree yielding its fruit every month. The leaves of the tree were for the healing of the nations. And there shall be no more curse, but the throne of God and of the Lamb shall be in it, and His servants shall serve Him. They shall see His face, and His name shall be on their foreheads. There shall be no night there: They need no lamp nor light of the sun, for the Lord God gives them light. And they shall reign forever and ever."

The pure river of life will come from the throne of God and the Lamb, symbolizing eternal life. This gives us a prophetic picture of the fullness of life in eternity with God, and the eternal blessings that come from Him. John also describes a tree of life, which will produce twelve fruits, symbolically representing the twelve tribes of Israel and Messiah's twelve apostles. Just as the tree of life was in the middle of the Garden of Eden (Gen. 2:9), the tree of life in the New Jerusalem will be located in the middle of its street. All of the saints will be able to partake freely from the tree of life, because sin and death will have been destroyed (Rev. 20:14). In Genesis, God placed a cherubim and a flaming sword to guard the tree of life (Gen. 3:24). In the New Jerusalem, the tree of life will dwell among the saints, symbolizing eternal life!

Why are there leaves of healing for the nations? As we discovered in the last chapter, Messiah's millennial reign will have water flowing from the temple that produces trees with healing leaves

(Ezek. 47:12). John is not indicating that there will be a need of healing in the New Jerusalem, but implying that the water and tree of life symbolizes strength, health, and wellness. Additionally, in the very next sentence, he states, "there will be no more curse," confirming that the leaves are symbolic for strength and wellness. Let us remember, in the New Jerusalem, there will be no more death, sorrow, pain, or illness (Rev. 21:4).

In one of the most anticipated and exciting events for all of the saints, we will see God's face! Throughout the history of the world, no one has seen God Almighty's face. Why? All of mankind is morally imperfect, corruptible, and finite (1 Cor. 15:50–58), and thus cannot see the holiness and perfection of God Almighty and continue to live.

Exodus 33:20, But He said, "You cannot see My face; for no man shall see Me, and live."

John 1:18, "No one has seen God at any time."

In the New Jerusalem, when all of the saints are incorruptible, immortal, and without sin, we will finally be able to see God's face! All of the human minds throughout history cannot comprehend the incredible magnitude of this awesome event. We will be blessed to see God Almighty's face, and His name will be on our foreheads. The saints will live in the presence of God Almighty and the Lamb, Messiah, forever and ever! Amen! Hallelujah!

CHAPTER 12

MESSIAH'S FINAL WARNING

In the most famous prophetic sermon of the Holy Bible, the Olivet Discourse, Messiah proclaims His final warning to mankind. He gives us great wisdom, knowledge, and understanding of the signs and events that will occur at the end of the age, shortly before His Second Coming. As we complete our journey on God's prophetic timeline, Messiah's final warning will confirm and verify that we are living at the end of the age. Now, without further delay, let us explore the final warning, the Olivet Discourse.

> Matthew 24:3–5, "Now as He sat on the Mount of Olives, the disciples came to Him privately, saying, "Tell us, when will these things be? And what will be the sign of Your coming, and of the end of the age?" And Jesus answered and said to them: "Take heed that no one deceives you. For many will come in My name, saying, 'I am the Christ,' and will deceive many."

On the Mount of Olives, the disciples privately asked Messiah for wisdom about the end of the age and His Second Coming. Messiah's first response was, "do not be deceived." Messiah's first warning of the end of the age warns us about the false prophets that will rise to deceive many people, including the greatest deceiver of all, the Antichrist. As we look around the world today, we can definitely recognize the false prophets who deny that Messiah came in the flesh, and also the false prophets who preach a corrupt, prosperity-focused, self-righteous, lukewarm, non-biblical gospel. Messiah warns us about these churches in the book of Revelation (Rev. 2–3). Certainly, this is the influence of the spirit of the Antichrist.

1 John 2:18, "Little children, it is the last hour; and as you have heard that the Antichrist is coming, even now many antichrists have come, by which we know that it is the last hour."

1 John 4:2–3, "By this you know the Spirit of God: Every spirit that confesses that Jesus Christ has come in the flesh is of God, and every spirit that does not confess that Jesus Christ has come in the flesh is not of God. And this is the spirit of the Antichrist, which you have heard was coming, and is now already in the world." (2 Pet. 2; 2 John 1:7–9)

Ever since the fall of man (Gen. 3), there has always been an Antichrist (Satan) spirit in the world, and it will continue until Messiah conquers all kingdoms, dominions, rulers, authorities, and death, putting these things under His feet. Then, He will give the kingdom to the Father, God Almighty, who will be all in all (1 Cor. 15:24–28; Eph. 1:7–12)! Messiah continues to explain the signs and events that will occur at the end of the age.

Matthew 24:6–8, "And you will hear of wars and rumors of wars. See that you are not troubled; for all these things must come to pass, but the end is not yet. For nation will rise against nation, and kingdom against kingdom. And there will be famines, pestilences, and earthquakes in various places. *All these are the beginning of sorrows.*"

Messiah declares that once we see wars, famines, pestilences, and earthquakes, the *beginning of sorrows* has begun, but the end is not yet. Now, let us review each of these warning signs beginning with the wars.

Modern Day Map

WARS

Although there are nations who are at war across the globe, I believe Messiah is primarily speaking of the wars in the Middle East and North Africa areas (Egypt, Libya, and Sudan), which is the primary focus of His Second Coming. Messiah proclaims, "kingdom shall rise against kingdom," which is a direct reference to Daniel's four kingdoms that will rise on the Earth: the Babylonian Empire (Iraq), the Medo-Persian Empire (Iran), the Grecian Empire (Turkey), and the Antichrist's kingdom (conglomerate of all three kingdoms). As we discovered in the previous chapters, all of these kingdoms (land area) are in the Middle East and North Africa, and will "conquer" one another (kingdom against kingdom).

When we take a look at the Middle East and North Africa, since the fall of the Babylonian Empire (Saddam Hussein) in 2003, Iraq has been in a civil war, as Medo-Persia (Iran) and ISIS fight for power and control over the oil enriched country. Medo-Persia

(Iran) has also invaded Yemen,[1] and its deadly eyes are set on Saudi Arabia (Isa. 21). In Syria, a civil war has been ongoing since 2011–2012, and the superpowers of the world have joined the strategic battle, including, America, Russia, Iran (Medo-Persia), Turkey, Saudi Arabia (all countries of the North Thunder alliance), and China.[2]

In 2011, Egypt had an internal revolution, and the government changed leadership twice in one year.[3] Furthermore, the Second Sudanese Civil War is a conflict that began in 1983, and it continues as of this writing between the central Sudanese government and the Sudan People's Liberation Army.[4] In 2011, Libyan dictator Muammar Gaddafi was removed from leadership and killed, and Libya has been in a civil war ever since.[5] An interesting fact is that Egypt, Libya, and Sudan are the three countries that the Antichrist will conquer during the seven-year tribulation period (Dan. 11:43). Are they being "arranged" for his arrival?

As we journey on God's prophetic timeline from 1948 until Messiah's Second Coming and millennial reign, clearly, nations have risen against nations and kingdoms against kingdoms, including Daniel's prophesied kingdoms.

FAMINES

Just as Messiah warned, famines have definitely increased in their severity since the fulfillment of the 1948 prophecy. Please note, the numbers are estimates, because the researched data gives a range of numbers to evaluate. The purpose is to give an approximate idea of the increased deaths caused by famines around the world since 1948. From 441 BC to 1947 (2,388 years), there have been approximately 237 million people killed in various places around the world from famines (99,246/year). From 1948 until 2016 (68 years), there have been approximately 29 million people (428,485/year) who have been killed because of famines, with the following being the worst incidents:

- The Great Chinese Famine - 1959–1961 - 20 Million

- Famine of Cambodia -1975–1979- 2 Million

- North Korea Famine – 1996 - 2 Million

- Famine of the Republic of Congo - 1998–2004 - 3.8 Million[6]

Again, these are not exact numbers, only estimates, but it shows how many people on average per year have died because of famines. This is exactly what Messiah warned would happen in the Olivet Discourse.

PESTILENCES

Since the fulfillment of the 1948 prophecy, pestilences have become a global pandemic. We will discover a few of the viruses and how they have impacted mankind.

HIV/AIDS

In the early 1980s, HIV/AIDS became infamously recognized in the world as an epidemic for mankind. As of 2014, 37 million people have HIV worldwide. In 2014 alone, 1.2 million people died from the disease.[7] Sub-Saharan Africa, South Africa, and South East Asia are the regions most affected by HIV. America has approximately 1.2 million people living with HIV, which results in about 17,500 deaths per year.[8] Between 1981 and 2009, approximately 30 million people died worldwide from this global pandemic.

WEST NILE VIRUS

Although the West Nile Virus (WNV) was first identified in Uganda in 1937, approximately sixty years later in 1994, Algeria had the first major outbreak of the virus. Romania followed with a major outbreak of WNV as well in 1996. In 1999, WNV reached the shores of America (New York).[9] Since then, the epidemic has spread across the continental United States, into Canada, and southward into Latin America and the Caribbean islands.[10] As recently as 2012, a new strain of the virus was diagnosed in Italy.[11] It has also spread into Europe, Africa, Asia, Australia, the Middle East, and numerous other countries. Furthermore, in 2012, America had one of its worst epidemics when 286 people died in Texas.[12] As of 2016, the West Nile Virus is still a global pandemic.

BIRD FLU

In 2003, Avian influenza (Bird Flu) reached a pandemic level in Asia and spread throughout the continent. It reached Europe in 2005, and the Middle East and Africa in 2006.[13] According to World Health Organization, 359 human beings have died from Bird Flu in twelve countries across the world as of 2012.[14]

Other viruses have manifested themselves, as well, including Ebola, SARS, Hantavirus, Dengue fever, and the newest one to date, the Zika virus. In 2016, this pestilence significantly manifested in Puerto Rico, as the CDC estimates that 25 percent of the population will be infected by the Zika virus by years' end. The virus has also reached the shores of America, as over 600 people have been diagnosed with Zika in Florida.

Messiah prophesied that there would be pestilences at the end of the age, and all of these viruses are signs of Messiah's final warning.

EARTHQUAKES

Messiah warned that there would also be earthquakes in various places at the end of the age. Since 2001, there have been over four hundred earthquakes that have occurred on the Earth. They have manifested in various places all over the world, exactly as Messiah prophesied. Additionally, the earthquakes have occurred with greater magnitude than in the previous century. According to the Geological

Society of America, between 2004 and 2014, "18 earthquakes with magnitudes of 8.0 or more rattled subduction zones around the globe. That's an increase of 265 percent over the average rate of the previous century, which saw 71 great quakes."[15]

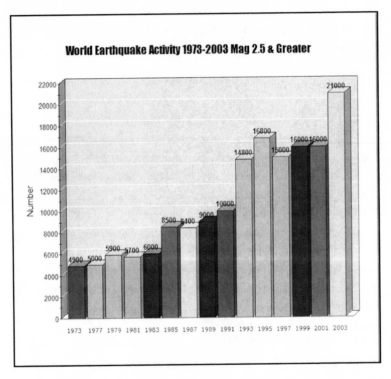

Mag 2.5- Mag 4-ANSS Composite Catalog 2007 by MWM, michaelmandeville. com[16]

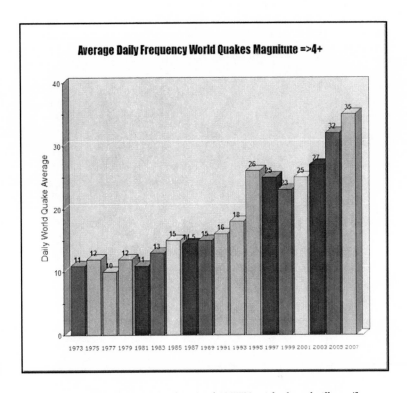

Mag 4-ANSS Composite Catalog 2007 by MWM, michaelmandeville.com[17]

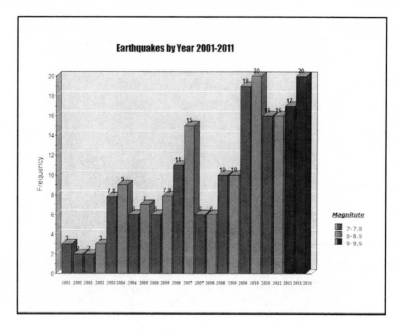

Earthquakes by year

As we can see, earthquakes have increased in velocity and magnitude. As we journey forward on God's prophetic timeline, we can be certain that these statistics will only increase before Messiah's Second Coming.

Have all of these warnings occurred on the Earth throughout history? Absolutely. However, Messiah is declaring that once we see these events occur simultaneously with more and more intensity, then we are living at the end of the age.

> Matthew 24:9–14, "Then they will deliver you up to tribulation and kill you, and you will be hated by all nations for My name's sake. And then many will be offended, will betray one another, and will hate one another. Then many false prophets will rise up and deceive many. And because

lawlessness will abound, the love of many will grow cold. But he who endures to the end shall be saved. And this gospel of the kingdom will be preached in all the world as a witness to all the nations, and then the end will come."

Since 1948, as wars, famines, pestilences, and earthquakes have occurred with more frequency and intensity, the elect and the saints have continued to be persecuted by the nations, including governments, because of their hatred for Messiah. As of today, with the rise of the terrorist organization known as ISIS, who is supported by Turkey (Grecian Empire) and Saudi Arabia, Jews and Christians, including women and children, have been the primary targets of these barbarians. Certainly, these terrorists have become the precursor to the Antichrist by delivering up believers and killing them. During the great tribulation, the Antichrist will advance the persecution to the highest level (Dan. 7:25), because he will understand that his time is short and he will be coming to an end (Rev. 12:12). Hallelujah!

Messiah also gives us great insight as to the culture of our world. He prophesies that, "many will be offended, the love of many will grow cold, and people will betray and hate one another, because lawlessness will abound" (2 Tim. 3:1–5). Does this look familiar in today's culture and society? The resounding answer is absolutely yes, because the world calls evil good and good evil (Isa. 5:20). Unless a person is living in denial of reality, clearly the Jews and Christians are being persecuted around the world at an all time high. Even in America, believers are being fined, imprisoned, and forced to either close their business or comply with the apostate blasphemous agenda of the US government. As Messiah prophesied, the persecution of Jews and Christians will progressively become worse as we enter the final years of the end of the age before Messiah's Second Coming.

Messiah also reemphasizes the danger of false prophets who will rise and deceive many people, which is clearly occurring in our society today. Another important revelation is that, "the gospel of the kingdom will be preached in all of the world, and then the end will come." With the technology of the internet and the travel capability of today's generation, we can be certain that this is definitely being fulfilled. Messiah gives believers comfort and encouragement during this time of tribulation when He proclaims, "But he who endures to the end shall be saved." Amen!

THE FINAL WARNING - THE GREAT TRIBULATION

> Matthew 24:15–16, "Therefore when you see the 'abomination of desolation,' spoken of by Daniel the prophet, standing in the holy place" (whoever reads, let him understand), "then let those who are in Judea flee to the mountains."

As Messiah continues His Olivet Discourse, He prophesies about an exact point on God's prophetic timeline when He refers to the abomination of desolation. This event will occur at the midpoint of the seven-year tribulation (the last three and a half years of the age), when the Antichrist will break the seven year peace agreement. This prophecy is also confirmed in the book of Daniel (Dan. 9:27, 11:31, 12:6–7).

Messiah warns the children of Israel (Jews) who are living in Jerusalem (Judea) during the tribulation period to flee to the mountains when they see the abomination of desolation by the Antichrist in the temple. As we discovered, they will flee to Petra, Jordan, the southern battlefront of Messiah's Second Coming (Isa. 34, 63:1–6). In Messiah's love, grace, and mercy, He warns the children of Israel and all of mankind about what will take place during those days. He also confirms that the worst persecution in the history of the world will take place after the abomination of desolation, which is the great tribulation, the last three and a half years of the age.

Matthew 24:21–22, "For then there will be great tribulation, such as has not been since the beginning of the world until this time, no, nor ever shall be. And unless those days were shortened, no flesh would be saved; but for the elect's sake those days will be shortened."

Messiah confirms that the great tribulation will be the most horrific time in the history of the world, because, "no flesh would be saved if those days were not shortened." Please review Revelation chapters 12 through 19, which gives great understanding of the judgments of the last three and a half years of the age. However, for the elect's sake and for the fulfillment of the Scriptures, Messiah will return for His Second Coming. As Messiah continues, He warns us for the third time about the false prophets who will rise at the end of the age.

Matthew 24:23–26, "Then if anyone says to you, 'Look, here is the Christ!' or 'There!' do not believe it. For false christs and false prophets will rise and show great signs and wonders to deceive, if possible, even the elect. See, I have told you beforehand. "Therefore if they say to you, 'Look, He is in the desert!' do not go out; or 'Look, He is in the inner rooms!' do not believe it."

In the Olivet Discourse, which is Messiah's final warning, one of Messiah's main emphasis is on false prophets, which includes the Antichrist and the False Prophet (Rev. 13). During the great tribulation, it is clear that there will be many false prophets who will rise to show great signs and wonders in order to deceive people as Messiah warns. Please note, at this point in Messiah's prophecy, He is speaking of the last three and a half years of the age (Dan. 7:25, 12:7), which coincides with John's warning of the Antichrist and the False Prophet during the great tribulation. Messiah and John are prophesying about the same person and the exact same period of time.

Revelation 13:3–4, "And all the world marveled and followed the beast. So they worshiped the dragon who gave authority to the beast; and they worshiped the beast, saying, "Who is like the beast? Who is able to make war with him?""

Revelation 13:12–17, "And he exercises all the authority of the first beast in his presence, and causes the earth and those who dwell in it to worship the first beast, whose deadly wound was healed. He performs great signs, so that he even makes fire come down from heaven on the earth in the sight of men. And he deceives those who dwell on the earth by those signs which he was granted to do in the sight of the beast, telling those who dwell on the earth to make an image to the beast who was wounded by the sword and lived."

At this point in the Olivet Discourse, Messiah shifts the prophecy to His glorious appearing. All of mankind on Earth, including rulers and kings, dominions, principalities, authorities, and forces in the heavenly realm, will understand the moment of truth! There will not be any question as to who is the King of Kings and Lord of Lords!

Matthew 24:27–30, "For as the lightning comes from the east and flashes to the west, so also will the coming of the Son of Man be. Immediately after the tribulation of those days the sun will be darkened, and the moon will not give its light; the stars will fall from heaven, and the powers of the heavens will be shaken. Then the sign of the Son of Man will appear in heaven, and then all the tribes of the earth will mourn, and they will see the Son of Man coming on the clouds of heaven with power and great glory."

At Messiah's Second Coming, He will be seen by all people, nations, and kingdoms of the Earth, as He comes through the clouds on a white horse with the armies of heaven (you and me)

(Rev. 19:11–16; Dan. 7:13–14). Make no mistake, the inhabitants on the earth will not have to tell anyone that the Lord of Lords and the King of Kings has arrived! Messiah describes how awesome and terrible that day will be as, "the sun will be darkened, the moon will not give its light, the stars will fall from heaven, and the powers of heaven will be shaken." This is the same language that the prophet Joel used in describing the great and terrible day of the Lord (See Joel 2:10–11, 30–32). The Day of the Lord will be an unbelievably awesome day for God's saints, and an absolutely horrific day for the unbelievers.

Now, let us understand the idioms associated with the Lord's trumpets that are found throughout the Holy Bible, because they give us great insight into Messiah's Second Coming events, as well.

- First Trump - The Feast of Shavuot (Pentecost)
- Last Trump - The Feast of Trumpets (Teruah)
- Great Trump - The Feast of Yom Kippur (Day of Israel's Atonement/Second Coming)

The idioms for the Lord's trumpets correlate with the feasts of the Lord (Lev. 23), which give us wisdom, knowledge, and understanding of the end time prophecies, including the book of Revelation. Now, let us discover the idioms found in the Olivet Discourse.

Matthew 24:31, "And He will send His angels with a *great sound of a trumpet*, and they will gather together His elect from the four winds, from one end of heaven to the other." (emphasis mine)

On the Lord's appointed year, and according to His idioms and feasts, Messiah's Second Coming will occur on the Feast of Yom Kippur, the Day of Atonement. Messiah declares, "He will send His angels with a great trump," referring us to the Feast of Yom Kippur (Lev. 23). Furthermore, the reference to the white linens and garments in Revelation 19 also symbolize the Feast of Yom Kippur, because we know that the Torah commanded the high priests to only wear all white on this specific day (Also see Lev. 16; Matt. 5:17–18).

> Revelation 19:11, 14, "Now I saw heaven opened, and behold, a white horse. And He who sat on him was called Faithful and True, and in righteousness He judges and makes war. *And the armies' in heaven, clothed in fine linen, white and clean, followed Him on white horses.*" (emphasis mine)

The Lord commanded the high priests in the Torah (Lev. 16) to clothe themselves in white linen garments, which symbolizes purity in order for them to make "atonement" for the children of Israel and for themselves. This was a prophetic foreshadow of Messiah's Second Coming with the purified saints from heaven on Yom Kippur. The prophet Joel gives us great understanding of this prophetic feast, as well.

> Joel 2:15–16, "*Blow the trumpet in Zion*, consecrate a fast, call a sacred assembly; Gather the people, sanctify the congregation, assemble the elders, gather the children and nursing babes; *Let the bridegroom go out from his chamber, and the bride from her dressing room.*" (emphasis mine)

The "fast day" directly refers to the Feast of Yom Kippur. If any Jewish person is asked what day "the fast day" occurs, the resounding answer would be Yom Kippur. Joel proclaims that on the fast day of Yom Kippur, "prepare the people and sanctify the congregation, because the bridegroom (Messiah) is coming from His chamber and the bride (believers) from her dressing room (Second Coming)!" This substantiates that Messiah's Second Coming will occur on God's appointed year on the Feast of Yom Kippur. Before we continue to explore the Olivet Discourse, it cannot be emphasized enough how important it is to have wisdom, knowledge, and understanding of the Lord's seven feasts (Lev. 23). Why?

First of all, the Lord commanded us to observe His feasts (Lev. 23), and secondly, Messiah clearly states that He is going to fulfill the Torah and the Prophets, including the seven feasts (Matt. 5:17–18). As we discovered, without the basic understanding of the idioms of His feasts (Lev. 23) and the knowledge of Messiah's traditions (Jewish), it is impossible to completely understand the Olivet Discourse or the book of Revelation. In summary, below are the seven feasts of the Lord (Leviticus 23), and what Hebrew date on God's calendar these prophetic events has and will be fulfilled on God's appointed year.

First Feast - Passover (crucified) Nisan 14 – Fulfilled

Second Feast - Unleavened Bread (buried) Nisan 15 – Fulfilled

Third Feast - First Fruits (resurrected) Nisan 16 – Fulfilled

Fourth Feast - Shavuot (The Holy Spirit poured out) – Fulfilled

Fifth Feast-Trumpets (Rapture/Seven-Year Tribulation/The Opening of the Books and Gates/Wedding of Messiah/ Coronation of Messiah) Tishri 1–2 – Unfulfilled

Sixth Feast - Yom Kippur (Second Coming) Tishri 10 – Unfulfilled

Seventh Feast - Tabernacles (Millennial Reign) Tishri 15 – 21 – Unfulfilled

Messiah fulfilled the first four feasts to the exact day, hour, and details of the ceremonies. So, if Messiah is the same yesterday, today, and forever (Heb. 13:8), and He does not change (Mal. 3:6), and He is going to fulfill "every jot and tittle" of the Torah and the Prophets (Matt. 5:17–18), then He will fulfill the Feast of Trumpets, the Feast of Yom Kippur, and the Feast of Tabernacles, as well! Messiah will also fulfill them in the exact order and according to their ceremonies in Leviticus 23. Please note, the events of the Feast of Trumpets could happen on different years in the seven-year tribulation, or on the same year. Nevertheless, they will occur on the Feast of Trumpets.

Now, let us discover the Jewish history and traditions of the Feast of Trumpets and discover how it became a two-day feast (Tishri 1–2). It is a two-day feast because of the Diaspora, or the scattering of the children of Israel among the nations after the destruction of Jerusalem by Nebuchadnezzar and the Babylonians (Jer. 25). This is the only feast that is celebrated on the new moon, which falls on Tishri 1 of the Hebrew calendar. Once the leaders knew on which day the new moon fell, they could mark the beginning of the Feast of Trumpets, as well as the other feasts that followed.

Since the children of Israel were exiled and scattered among the nations after the destruction of Jerusalem (586 BC), the only way they could communicate with each other and observe the Feast of Trumpets was by lighting fires on the mountaintops. Therefore, by the time they were able to spread the word and observe the Feast of Trumpets, the day was over. So, the Feast of Trumpets was observed for two days in order to ensure that all of the children of Israel could observe it, as commanded by God (Lev. 23). In Judaism, it is known as the "one long feast day," or the feast where, "no one would knew the day or the hour it came," because of the disbursement and the amount of time it took to light the fires on the mountaintops across the land.

Another tradition and customary terminology used by the children of Israel related to a Jewish wedding. In Jesus' day, weddings were arranged, so when someone would ask the son when his wedding day was, the son would say, "Only my father knows." Just as we have sayings and terminology in different parts of the world in which we live, according to Jewish tradition, this was a typical saying among the children of Israel. Let us remember, Jesus is a Jew and spoke in Aramaic, so when He spoke using these traditions and customary terminology, the children of Israel, including His disciples, would have understood its reference. With this in mind, let us discover these traditions as we continue Messiah's Olivet Discourse.

> Matthew 24:36–44, *"But of that day and hour no one knows, not even the angels of heaven, but My Father only.* But as the days of Noah were, so also will the coming of the Son of Man be. For as in the days before the flood, they were eating and drinking, marrying and giving in marriage, until the day that Noah entered the ark, and did not know until the flood came and took them all away, so also will the coming of the Son of Man be. Then two men will be in the field: one will be taken and the other left. Two women will be grinding at the mill: one will be taken and the other left. *Watch therefore*, for you do not know what hour your Lord is coming. *But know this*, that if the master of the house had known what hour the thief would come; he would have watched and not allowed his house to be broken into. Therefore, you also be ready, for the Son of Man is coming at an hour you do not expect." (emphasis mine)

Messiah is prophesying about the Rapture, as "one will be taken and one left." He is telling us that the Rapture will occur on the Feast of Trumpets (God's appointed year) when He states, "no one knows the day or hour" (from the tradition above). In Messiah's day, the disciples were very familiar with the Diaspora, because it was the event that caused this feast to be known as, "the feast that nobody knew the day or hour that it would come." So, when Messiah proclaims, "no one knows the day or hour," the disciples would have understood that He was speaking about the Feast of Trumpets. When Messiah states this tradition and uses this terminology, He is telling us that the Rapture will occur on God's appointed year on the Feast of Trumpets, either on Tishri 1 or Tishri 2. With that being said, since it occurs on Tishri 1 or Tishri 2, nobody will know the day or hour!

As Messiah concludes His prophecy of the Rapture, He gives us a parable about the master and the thief. One would think that if He did not want us to understand this feast and its events, He would not have given us this parable for our knowledge concerning the Rapture. Messiah would have just declared, "no one will know the time," and not include, "watch therefore" or "but know this" statements. Make no mistake, He does not want our heads to be buried in the sand, but instead, filled with knowledge, so that we understand His traditions and terminology. As Messiah continues, He gives us another parable that confirms He wants us to watch and to understand the "time of our visitation" (Also see Luke 19:41–44).

> Matthew 24:45–51, "Who then is a faithful and wise servant, whom his master made ruler over his household, to give them food in due season? Blessed is that servant whom his master, when he comes, will find so doing. Assuredly, I say to you that he will make him ruler over all his goods. But if that evil servant says in his heart, 'My master is delaying his coming,' and begins to beat his fellow servants, and to eat and drink with the drunkards, the master of that servant will come on a day when he is not looking for him and at an hour that he is not aware of, and will cut him in two and appoint his portion with the hypocrites. There shall be weeping and gnashing of teeth."

Messiah is clearly telling us that if we understand His seven feasts and the biblical prophecies of His Second Coming, and if we are watchful, then we will be faithful and wise servants. There is not any reason why Messiah would have given us two parables back to back concerning watching and understanding the signs of His return unless it was extremely imperative and wise to do so. In fact, Messiah ends this parable with very strong and rebuking language when He states that if a person does not watch, "He will cut him in two and appoint his portion to the hypocrites, where there is weeping and gnashing of teeth."

Let us remember why Messiah allowed the destruction of the city of Jerusalem and the temple at His First Coming. He allowed this event because, "the children of Israel did not understand the time of their visitation," which was His First Coming (Luke 19:41–44). Certainly, God wants us to understand "the time of our visitation," or He would not have given us the wise parables. On God's appointed year, the Rapture will occur on the Feast of Trumpets (Tishri 1 or 2). For more confirmation of Messiah's warning concerning not understanding the times of His Second Coming, please see Rev. 3:3, Matt. 16:3, and Luke 19:41–44.

THE PARABLE OF THE FIG TREE

> Matthew 24:32–35, "Now learn this parable from the fig tree: When its branch has already become tender and puts forth leaves, you know that summer is near. So you also, when you see all these things, know that it is near—at the doors! Assuredly, I say to you, this generation will by no means pass away till all these things take place. Heaven and earth will pass away, but My words will by no means pass away."

Messiah used a parable of a fig tree to give us great insight as to when the warnings of the Olivet Discourse will occur. Some Bible scholars and prophecy teachers believe that Messiah was prophesying about when Israel became a nation again, as Israel is symbolically represented as a fig tree in the Scriptures (Jer. 24). This view states that when Israel became a nation again in 1948, and when the warning signs of the Olivet Discourse begin to appear, then that generation would see Messiah's Second Coming.

However, as we discussed in chapter one, once the children of Israel recaptured Jerusalem as its capital (1967), and the Lord builds up the holy city (Psalms 102:16, 18), then that generation is the terminal generation. Please note, it is only a nineteen-year difference that should not dictate and influence us from watching and understanding what the Biblical prophets are telling us of today. Instead, we should focus our eyes on the prophecies of Daniel, and others, watching the kingdoms as they are dethroned from their power in the exact order prophesied.

THE PARABLE OF THE WISE AND FOOLISH VIRGINS

Matthew 25:1–13, "Then the kingdom of heaven shall be likened to ten virgins who took their lamps and went out to meet the bridegroom. *Now five of them were wise, and five were foolish.* Those who were foolish took their lamps and took no oil with them, but the wise took oil in their vessels with their lamps. But while the bridegroom was delayed, they all slumbered and slept. "And at midnight a cry was heard: 'Behold, the bridegroom is coming; go out to meet him!' Then all those virgins arose and trimmed their lamps. And the foolish said to the wise, 'Give us some of your oil, for our lamps are going out.' But the wise answered, saying, 'No, lest there should not be enough for us and you; but go rather to those who sell, and buy for yourselves.' And while they went to buy, the bridegroom came, and those who were ready went in with him to the wedding; and the door was shut. "Afterward the other virgins came also, saying, 'Lord, Lord, open to us!' But he answered and said, 'Assuredly, I say to you, I do not know you.' "*Watch therefore, for you know neither the day nor the hour in which the Son of Man is coming.*" (emphasis mine)

As Messiah continues His Olivet Discourse, He gives a third parable so that we can "understand the time of our visitation." Again, Messiah would not have given us three parables in the Olivet Discourse if He had not wanted us to understand the events of the end of the age and His Second Coming. Since the five wise virgins had prepared properly and watched faithfully, they were invited as guests of the bridegroom's (Messiah) wedding. However, the five foolish virgins in the parable did not prepare, nor did they watch, so they were not invited to Messiah's wedding! He told the foolish virgins, "assuredly, I say to you, I do not know you." Messiah ends the parable stating, "Watch therefore, for you know neither the day nor the hour in which the Son of Man is coming." He is referring believers who understand His Jewish traditions and terminology to the Feast of Trumpets, as this is when He will "rapture" His bride! The apostle Paul gives us great insight into the Rapture event, as well.

> 1 Corinthians 15:51–52, "Behold, I tell you a mystery: We shall not all sleep, but we shall all be changed—in a moment, in the twinkling of an eye, *at the last trumpet*. For the trumpet will sound, and the dead will be raised incorruptible, and we shall be changed."(emphasis mine) (Also see 1 Thess. 4:16).

Paul also confirms that the Rapture will occur on the Feast of Trumpets. Remember, as we discussed, the "last trump" is the Feast of Trumpets (Great Trump is Yom Kippur-Second Coming).

THE FINAL WARNING, THE GREAT COMMISSION

As Messiah continues His prophetic sermon, He gives us yet another parable for our wisdom and understanding. In this parable, He compares the kingdom of heaven to a master who had loaned money to his servants before he went on a journey.

> Matthew 25:14–19, "For the kingdom of heaven is like a man traveling to a far country, who called his own servants

and delivered his goods to them. And to one he gave five talents, to another two, and to another one, to each according to his own ability; and immediately he went on a journey. Then he who had received the five talents went and traded with them, and made another five talents. And likewise he who had received two gained two more also. But he who had received one went and dug in the ground, and hid his lord's money. After a long time, the lord of those servants came and settled accounts with them."

The master went on a far journey, and he gave each servant a quantity of talents, according to the ability of each servant. The first two servants invested their talents and doubled the amount of talents that the master had given them when he left on his journey. However, the third servant did not invest his talent, but instead, he coveted it and buried it in the ground. After some time, the master returned home to settle the accounts with them.

Matthew 25:20–23, "So he who had received five talents came and brought five other talents, saying, 'Lord, you delivered to me five talents; look, I have gained five more talents besides them.' His lord said to him, 'Well done, good and faithful servant; you were faithful over a few things, I will make you ruler over many things. Enter into the joy of your lord.' He also who had received two talents came and said, 'Lord, you delivered to me two talents; look, I have gained two more talents besides them.' His lord said to him, 'Well done, good and faithful servant; you have been faithful over a few things, I will make you ruler over many things. Enter into the joy of your lord.'"

Once the master returned to settle the accounts with his servants, the first two servants received praise, honor, and glory, because they were not lazy and worked. They compounded the talents into double the amount that their master had given them. The master told them, "Well done, good and faithful servant," and he set both of them as rulers over many things in the kingdom. However, the third servant who coveted his talent, was greeted with a completely different reward.

> Matthew 25:24–27, "Then he who had received the one talent came and said, 'Lord, I knew you to be a hard man, reaping where you have not sown, and gathering where you have not scattered seed. And I was afraid, and went and hid your talent in the ground. Look, there you have what is yours.' "But his lord answered and said to him, '*You wicked and lazy servant,* you knew that I reap where I have not sown, and gather where I have not scattered seed. So you ought to have deposited my money with the bankers, and at my coming I would have received back my own with interest."

The third servant with one talent was wicked, lazy, and reluctant to increase his talent, so he saved it. The lazy and wicked servant did not please the master and did not do his will, because he did not even earn interest on the talent that was given to him. The master tells us the lazy servant's reward for his disobedience.

> Matthew 25:28–29, "Therefore take the talent from him, and give it to him who has ten talents." 'For to everyone who has, more will be given, and he will have abundance; but from him who does not have, even what he has will be taken away. And cast the unprofitable servant into the outer darkness. There will be weeping and gnashing of teeth.'"

As judgment for his wickedness, the master took the lazy servant's talent and gave it to the servant with ten talents. The third servant, who was wicked and lazy, did not fulfill his duty to the master, and he was cast into outer darkness where there is weeping and gnashing of teeth. What can we learn from the "loaned money" parable?

Messiah's parable about the loaned money is a great lesson for all of mankind. However, this parable is not about money, but rewards in the kingdom of heaven. It is a parable about the Great Commission (Matt. 28:19–20), which tells all of mankind, including believers, to use our God-given spiritual gifts, abilities, and talents to do Messiah's will for our life and bring glory to His kingdom! When we enter into Messiah's eternal kingdom, we will be rewarded for our labor (talent). Please note, when the master proclaimed, "Well done, good and faithful servant," he did not say anything about money, but instead declared, "I will make you ruler over many things." Certainly, this is a clear reference to the kingdom of heaven, since we will receive Messiah's rewards (ruler of many things) for what we have done with what God has blessed us with (talents).

If we multiply our spiritual gifts and talents by doing our part for Messiah's kingdom on Earth, then we will receive our rewards in heaven, and we will become rulers over many things! On the contrary, if we do not, then we will be cast into hell, where there will be weeping and gnashing of teeth, just as the wicked lazy servant experienced. The choice is ours!

Of course, we are to be responsible with our money and use it for God's purposes, because He has blessed us with it. However, this parable is about being the salt of the earth and the light of the world (Great Commission) and working God's harvest. In doing so, we will multiply our talents!

Matthew 5:13–16, "You are the salt of the earth. But if the salt loses its saltiness, how can it be made salty again? It is no longer good for anything, except to be thrown out and trampled underfoot. "You are the light of the world. A town built on a hill cannot be hidden. Neither do people light a lamp and put it under a bowl. Instead they put it on its stand, and it gives light to everyone in the house. In the same way, let your light shine before others, that they may see your good deeds and glorify your Father in heaven."

Matthew 28:19–20, "Go therefore and make disciples of all the nations, baptizing them in the name of the Father and of the Son and of the Holy Spirit, teaching them to observe all things that I have commanded you; and lo, I am with you always, even to the end of the age."

Luke 12:48, "For everyone to whom much is given, from him much will be required."

Luke 17:33, "Whoever seeks to save his life will lose it, and whoever loses his life will preserve it."

Matthew 9:37–38, "Then He said to His disciples, "The harvest truly is plentiful, but the laborers are few. Therefore, pray the Lord of the harvest to send out laborers into His harvest."

It is very important to understand that it does not matter who we are, where we are from, how much money we have, what occupation we hold, or any other worldly status; if we use our God-given spiritual gifts (talents) and do God's will for His kingdom, we will be rewarded where it counts, in the kingdom of God! He only commands us to love Him with all of our heart, soul, mind, and strength (Matt. 22:37), trust and obey, not be lazy, and influence the people in our environment in a godly way. A great example of Messiah's "loaned money parable" is what He stated in the book of Mark concerning the poor widow.

Mark 12:41–44, "Now Jesus sat opposite the treasury and saw how the people put money into the treasury. And many who were rich put in much. Then one poor widow came and threw in two mites, which make a quadrans. So He called

His disciples to Himself and said to them, "Assuredly, I say to you that this poor widow has put in more than all those who have given to the treasury; for they all put in out of their abundance, but she out of her poverty put in all that she had, her whole livelihood." (Also see Matt. 19:16–30)

THE FINAL WARNING OF JUDGMENT ON THE NATIONS

Matthew 25:31–33, "When the Son of Man comes in His glory, and all the holy angels with Him, then He will sit on the throne of His glory. All the nations will be gathered before Him, and He will separate them one from another, as a shepherd divides his sheep from the goats. And He will set the sheep on His right hand, but the goats on the left."

As Messiah concludes His final warning during His Olivet Discourse, He prophesies about His judgment upon the nations. This will occur at His Second Coming, as He states, "when the Son of Man comes in His glory, He will sit on the throne of His glory," which is referring to David's everlasting throne. In the Davidic Covenant, God promised David that his throne would be everlasting, and that "the fruit of his body" will reign from his throne (2 Sam. 7:10–11; Ps. 132:11). Messiah will fulfill the Davidic Covenant at His Second Coming and millennial reign when He sits on David's throne in Jerusalem (2 Sam. 7:10–16; Isa. 9:6–7; Jer. 23:5–8, 19–26; Ps. 89:34–3; Acts 2:29–3; Rev. 22:16). At that time, He will divide the nations into sheep and goats. The sheep, which are the good nations, will be on His right, and the goats, which are the evil nations, will be on His left.

Matthew 25:34–40, "Then the King will say to those on His right hand (sheep), 'Come, you blessed of My Father, inherit the kingdom prepared for you from the foundation of the world: for I was hungry and you gave Me food; I was thirsty and you gave Me drink; I was a stranger and you took Me in; I was naked and you clothed Me; I was sick and you visited Me; I was in prison and you came to Me. Then the righteous will answer Him, saying, 'Lord, when did we see You hungry and feed You, or thirsty and give You drink? When did we see You a stranger and take You in, or naked and clothe You? Or when did we see You sick, or in prison, and come to You?' And the King will answer and say to them, 'Assuredly, I say to you, inasmuch as you did it to one of the least of these My brethren, you did it to Me.'"

Messiah tells us that the sheep, which are the nations who blessed His brethren, will inherit the kingdom of God. Please note, when Messiah speaks of the *elect*, He is speaking of the children of Israel, His brethren. Messiah is clearly warning the nations as to how they are to treat His heritage and His land of Israel (Joel 3:2). The nations who treat His brethren well and are not involved in dividing the Promised Land will inherit the kingdom of God. What about the goats?

Matthew 25:41–46, "Then He will also say to those on the left hand, 'Depart from Me, you cursed, into the everlasting fire prepared for the devil and his angels: for I was hungry and you gave Me no food; I was thirsty and you gave Me no drink; I was a stranger and you did not take Me in, naked and you did not clothe Me, sick and in prison and you did not visit Me.' Then they also will answer Him, saying, 'Lord, when did we see You hungry or thirsty or a stranger or naked or sick or in prison, and did not minister to You?' Then He will answer them, saying, 'Assuredly, I say to you, inasmuch as you did not do it to one of the least of these, you did not do it to Me.' And these will go away into everlasting punishment, but the righteous into eternal life."

On the contrary, Messiah will tell the goat nations to depart from Him, and they will be sent into the everlasting lake of fire and brimstone. The goat nations did not bless Messiah's brethren, the children of Israel, and they will receive everlasting punishment. This is a clear and final warning to all nations on the earth, including America, to treat the children of Israel as "brethren," and to not be a part of the division of the Promised Land (Joel 3:2).

> Genesis 12:3. "I will bless those who bless you, and I will curse him who curses you."

CONCLUSION

Messiah's final warning, the Olivet Discourse, gives us wisdom, knowledge, and understanding of the prophetic events that will occur after the 1948 and 1967 fulfilled prophecies until Messiah's Second Coming, which includes; the Antichrist's and False prophet's roles, the great tribulation, the fulfillment of the fall feasts including the Rapture and the seven-year tribulation (Trumpets), Messiah's Second Coming (Yom Kippur), His millennial reign (Tabernacles), the judgment of the sheep and the goats, and all of the signs of His Second Coming events. Without question, when we look around the world today, it is very apparent that the signs of the Olivet Discourse are beginning to be fulfilled (Matt. 24:7), and we have entered the "beginning of sorrows" (Matt. 24:8). According to God's prophetic timeline, which are prophecies by Messiah and the prophets, our generation is currently living in the Medo-Persian Empire (Iran), and the Grecian Empire (Turkey) is rising to power to conquer and destroy them (Dan. 2, 7, 8). Keep your eyes on Erdogan and Turkey, as the Grecian Empire is the next kingdom to be fulfilled after the Medo-Persian Empire. The final questions that remain are, "Are you paying attention to the signs of the end of the age? Will you recognize the time of our visitation?"

GOD'S PROPHETIC TIMELINE – THE SUMMARY OF THE SECOND COMING EVENTS:

- 1948/1967 Prophecies-Fulfilled

DANIEL 2

- Babylonian Empire (Iraq) - Fulfilled
- Medo-Persian Empire (Iran) > 2016
- Grecian Empire (Turkey)
- Antichrist's Kingdom

DANIEL 7

- Babylonian Empire (Iraq) - Fulfilled
- Medo-Persian Empire (Iran) > 2016
- Grecian Empire (Turkey)
- Antichrist's Kingdom

DANIEL 8

- Medo-Persian Empire (Iran) - Coincides with Daniel 2 and Daniel 7's second beast > 2016
- Grecian Empire (Turkey) - Coincides with Daniel 2 & Daniel 7's third beast
- The Antichrist (little horn, 10 Kings)- Coincides with Daniel 2 & Daniel 7's fourth beast

SECOND COMING EVENTS

- Rapture/Seven-Year Tribulation - The Feast of Trumpets

(Rapture will occur and the Seven-Year Tribulation will begin, Rev. 6 through 19)

- Second Coming – The Feast of Yom Kippur (Rev. 19)
- Millennial Reign-The Feast of Tabernacles (Rev. 20)
- End of the Millennial Reign before the New Jerusalem - Great White Throne Judgment - (individual judgment of all non-believers, Rev. 20)
- New Jerusalem- The Feast of Tabernacles (Rev. 21–22)

My friends, we live in the most exciting times since the First Coming of Messiah! Do you realize how many believers in the last two thousand years would have loved to live in these prophetic times of today, in order to witness the fulfillment of the Biblical prophecies that were written over 2,500 years ago, and by Moses over 3,500 years ago? And guess what? God has specifically chosen you and me to live in these awesome, prophetic times, so that we can be the light of the world and the salt of the earth (Matt. 5:13–16) and proclaim the Good News of Messiah, including the Biblical prophecies and His glorious appearing (Second Coming)! Please remember, "for the testimony of Jesus, is the spirit of prophecy (Rev. 19:10).

Who can dispute that over 2,500 years ago Isaiah prophesied that Israel would become a nation again in 1948 (Isa. 66:8)? Who can dispute the prophet who prophesied that the children of Israel would recapture Jerusalem after two thousand years of exile, and the Lord would build up Zion?

As of 2016, who can dispute that we are witnessing the fulfillment of Daniel 2, 7, and 8, which are the prophesied kingdoms that will rise at the time of the end, the end of the age before Messiah's Second Coming? God's prophetic timeline is occurring right before our eyes!

Always remember, God is on His everlasting throne, controlling everything and everybody, including Satan, so we are not to have a spirit of fear, but of strength and courage (Joshua 1:9). I pray that you will be a "wise virgin" and not a "foolish virgin," and keep your lamps filled with oil (Matt. 25), watching and waiting for the Lion of Judah to return!

In the name higher than every other name, Yeshua (Jesus), the Messiah, the King of Israel, the King of Kings, and the Lord of Lords, the eternal and everlasting God of Abraham, Isaac, and Jacob! Amen, Amen, and Amen!

> Luke 21:28, "Now when these things begin to happen, look up and lift up your heads, because your redemption draws near."

> Revelation 22:20–21, "He who testifies to these things says, "Surely I am coming quickly." Amen. Even so, come, Lord Jesus! The grace of our Lord Jesus Christ be with you all. Amen."

EPILOGUE

Messiah's final warning has been proclaimed, and God's prophetic timeline is like sand through an hour glass as it reaches its final destination. Now, the question is, "Have God's fishermen and Satan's hunters been released?"

In our upcoming book, *God's Fishermen, Satan's Hunters*, we will explore this incredible prophecy in the Holy Bible and discover the profound answers as it correlates with the events of today!

ENDNOTES

CHAPTER FOUR: THE PEOPLE OF THE PRINCE WHO IS TO COME

1. Tacitus, *The History* New Ed edition Book 5.1 Editor: Moses Hadas, Translators: Alfred Church, William Brodribb (Modern Library; New York, 2003).

2. Flavius Josephus, The Complete Works of Josephus, The Wars Of The Jews Or The History Of The Destruction Of Jerusalem Book III, Chapter 1, Paragraph 3.

3. Flavius Josephus, *The Complete Works of Josephus*, The Wars of the Jews Or The History Of The Destruction Of Jerusalem Trans. William Whiston BOOK II: CHAPTER 13: Paragraph 7.

4. Flavius Josephus, *The Complete Works of Josephus*, The Wars of the Jews Or The History Of The Destruction of Jerusalem Book III, Chapter 4, Paragraph 20.

5. Flavius Josephus, The Complete Works of Josephus, The Wars of the Jews Or The History Of The Destruction of Jerusalem Trans. William Whiston, BOOK V; Chapter 13, Paragraph 4.

6. Pace, H. Geva, "The Camp of the Tenth Legion in Jerusalem: An Archeological Reconsideration," IEJ 34 (1984), pp. 247-249.

CHAPTER FIVE: NEBUCHADNEZZAR'S STATUE DREAM

1. Rome and Parthia at War, March 2006. All Empires, Online History Community Http://www.allempires. com.
2. Justin's History of the World as cited in Trogus Pompeius, in Justin, Cornelius Nepos and Eutropius, John Selby Watson, tr. (London: George Bell and Sons, 1876), pp. 272–28.3

CHAPTER SIX: WHAT KINGDOM IS OUR GENERATION LIVING IN TODAY?

1. Lawrence Rothfield (1 Aug 2009). The Rape of Mesopotamia: Behind the Looting of the Iraq Museum. University of Chicago Press.
2. BBC News, Andrew North, November 14, 2008.
3. Find God in Bible Prophecy: Rebuilding Babylon, Dianne E. Butts, June 27, 2012, http;//www.findinggoddaily.com.
4. Lawrence Freedman and Efraim Karsh, The Gulf Conflict: Diplomacy and War in the New World Order, 1990–1991 (Princeton, 1993), 331–41.
5. AP News Archive; Excerpts From Saddam's Speech with Am-Gulf RDP, BJT, January 6, 1991.
6. Iran's Top Leader Undergoes Prostate Surgery, New York Times September 8, 2014. Thomas Erdbrink.
7. Iran's supreme leader Ayatollah Ali Khamenei has prostate surgery. The Guardian. September 8, 2014.
8. *Le Figaro* quoted Western intelligence officials as saying that the cancer was discovered about ten years ago. 2/27/2015. Philippe Gelie.

9. Ahmari, Sohrab (March 22,2015). "Iran's Coming Leadership Crisis". Wall Street Jounal: A13.

10. "The 72 Who Rule the World," *Forbes.* The World's Most Powerful People. Kathryn Dill November 4, 2015.

11. Gokay, Bulent, Xypolia, IIia (2013). Reflections on Taksim-Gezi Park Protests in Turkey (PDF). *Journel of Global Faultlines.*

12. Arsu, Sebnem (4 June 2013). "Turkish Official Apologizes for Force Used at Start of Riots" *The New York Times.*

13. "1,863 Turkish journalists fired during AKP rule, opposition report says" Hurriyet Daily News. 27 October 2014.

14. Oktem, Kerem (10 June 2013). "Why Turkey's mainstream media chose to show penguins rather than protests," *The Guardian.*

15. Erdogan approves law tightening Turkey's Internet controls." Reuters. 12 September 2014.

16. "Turkey Blocks Twitter." *The Washington Post.* 21 March 2014.

17. Candar, Cengiz (2014-02-24). "The Erdogan tapes." al-Monitor.

18. Roy Gutman (6 February 2014). "Erdogan recordings appear real, analyst says, as Turkey scandal grows" Sacramento Bee.

19. Kevin Rawlinson (2014-03-20). "Turkey blocks use of Twitter after prime minister attacks social media site." The Guardian.

20. Constanze Letsch (21 March 2014). "Turkey Twitter uses flout Erdogan ban on micro-blogging site" The Guardian.

21. Emre Peker (3 June 2014). "Turkey Lifts Ban on YouTube Access". *The Wall Street Journal.*

22. Turkey's Erdogan warns top court after ruling on detained journalists (www.reuters.com, 11 March 2016).

23. "Erdogan approves law tightening Turkey's Internet controls." Reuters. 12 September 2014.

24. "Turkish PM: Israel is the main threat to Mideast peace." Haaretz.com.

25. Report: Turkish PM Erdogan says 'Palestine today is an open-air prison.'" Haaretz. 1 January 2009.

26. Ben Solomon, Ariel (14 July 2014). "Erdogan accuses Israel of 'using terrorism' in its operations against Hamas in Gaza. *The Jerusalem Post.*

27. "Erdogan accuses Israel of deliberately killing Palestinian mothers" Haartz.com.

28. "Turkish Prime Minister says Israel is 'more barbaric than Hitler.'" *The Independent.* 20 July 2014.

29. Walid Shoebat, December 31, 2015, Http://www.shoebat.com.

30. YourNewswire.com, by Sean Adl-Tabatabal. "Erdogan becomes dictator of Turkey, Purging 20,000 'Traitor citizens.'" Accessed July 18,2016.

31. CNN, Ivan Watson and Mohamed Fadel Fahmy, September 14, 2011.

32. *The Express Tribune*, "Iranians are 'not Muslims', says top Saudi cleric." By AFP, September 6, 2016.

33. *The Express Tribune*, "Iranians are 'not Muslims', says top Saudi cleric." By AFP, September 6, 2016.

34. Nicola Slawson, January 2, 2016, *The Guardian.*

35. Iran Front Page, "Iran strongly condemns execution of Sheikh Nimr," January 2, 2016.

36. *USA Today*, Gregg Zoroya, January 3, 2016

37. Gulf News, Saudi Arabia, "Northern Thunder military exercises begin in Saudi Arabia." May 25, 2016.

38. Arab News, "North Thunder" sends a message of unity, power, February 17, 2006.
39. Ibid.
40. Ibid.
41. "Today Major Prophecy Was Fulfilled. The Date August 24th Is Prophetically Significant For Muslims Worldwide Sparking Islam's Caliphate Empire And Is Why Turkey Today Sent A Massive Land Invasion To Syria." by Walid Shoebat. http://shoebat.com/author/walid-shoebat/.
42. Assyrian International News Agency, Report: Seized USB Drives Reveal Turkey's Links to ISIL, July 27, 2015.
43. Ibid.

CHAPTER 7: THE ANTICHRIST'S KINGDOM

1. Gibbons, *The Decline And Fall Of The Roman Empire.*

CHAPTER 8: MYSTERY BABYLON THE GREAT, THE MOTHER OF HARLOTS

1. Bernard Lewis, *The Arabs in History*, page 15, B. L London 1947.
2. "Saudi pumps up oil production to record high 10.3 million bpd. Reuters. 8 April 2015.
3. "Rights Group condemns Saudi beheadings" Associated Press.
4. Andrea Dworkin (1978). A feminist Looks at Saudi Arabia. Andrea Dworkin on nostatusquo.com.
5. Green, Chris (17 March 2016). "PR firm accused of helping Saudi Arabia 'whitewash' its human rights record." *The Independent.*

6. Saeed, Abdullah; Saeed, Hassan (2004). *Freedom of Religion, Apostasy and Islam.* Ashgate Publishing. P.227. ISBM 0-7546-3083-8.

7. "Saudi Arabia's New Law Imposes Death Sentence for Bible Smugglers?" Christian Post.

CHAPTER 12: MESSIAH'S FINAL WARNING

1. Al Jazeera, "Saudi Arabia, Iran and the 'Great Game' in Yemen, by Martin Reardon, 26 March 2015.

2. International conflict. "Iran to join, Russia already bombing Opposition's positions." Reuters.com. Reuters.

3. Korotayev A. Zinkina J. Egyptian Revolution: A Demographic Structural Analysis. Entelequia. Interdisiplinar 13 (2011):139-169.

4. "The descent into civil war." *The Economist.* 27 December 2013.

5. "Gaddafi killed as Libya's revolt claims hometown". Reuters Africa. 20 October 2011.

6. Wikipedia.org, List of Famines.

7. HIV/AIDS Fact Sheet N. WHO. November 2015.

8. Centers for Disease Control and Prevention, (CDC) (June 3,2011). "HIV surveillance, United States, 1981-2008". MMWR. Morbidity and mortality weekly report 60 (21):689-93. PMID 21637182.

9. Nash D, Mostashari F, Fine A, et al. (June 2001). "The outbreak of West Nile virus infection in the New York city area in 1999". N. Engl. J. Med. 344 (24): 1807-14. Doi:10.1056/ NEJM200106143442401. PMID 11407341.

10. Chen, Chen C.; Jenkins, Emily; Epp, Tasha; Waldner, Cheryl; Curry, Philip S.; Soos, Catherine (2013-07-22). "Climate Change and West Nile Virus in a Highly Endemic Region of North America". International Journal of Environmental Research and Public Health 10 (7): 3052-3071. Doi:10.3390/ijerph10073052. PMC 3734476. PMID 23880729.

11. Barzon L, Pacenti M, Franchin E, Lavezzo E, Martello T, Squarzon L, Toppo S, Fiorin F, Marchiori G, Russo F, Cattai M, Cusinato R, Palu G (2012). "New endemic West Nile virus lineage 1a in northern Italy, July 2012". Euro Surveillance: Bulletin Europeen Sur Les Maladies Transmissibles=European Communicable Disease Bulletin 17 (31). PMID 22874456.

12. Murray KO, Rukanonchai D, Hesalroad D, Fonken E, Nolan MS (November 2013). "West Nile virus, Texas, USA, 2012". Emerging Infectious Diseases 19 (11): 1836-8. Doi:10.3201/eid1911.130768. PMC 3837649. PMID 24210089.

13. "H5N1 avian influenza: Timeline of major events." World Health Organization. 25 Jan 2012.

14. NBC NEWS, Linda Carroll, 25 October 2014.

15. MWM Neil-PDE, World Earthquake Database, maintained by U.S. Geological Survey.

16. ANSS Composite Catalog 2007 by MWM, michaelmandeville.com

17. Ibid.

CPSIA information can be obtained
at www.ICGtesting.com
Printed in the USA
LVOW11s0808180717
541721LV00001B/62/P

9 781944 212445